W9-AJB-503

LOW-MAINTENANCE
WATER GARDENS

HELEN NASH

Sterling Publishing Co., Inc.
New York

Library of Congress Cataloging-in-Publication Data

Nash, Helen, 1944–
    Low-maintenance water gardens   /   Helen Nash.
        p.   cm.
    Includes index.
    ISBN 0-8069-4886-8
    1. Water gardens.   2. Low maintenance gardening.   I. Title.
SB423.N365   1996
635.9′674 — dc20   96-13595
                                                                       CIP

Photography by Oliver Jackson

Designed by Judy Morgan

3 5 7 9 10 8 6 4

First paperback edition published in 1998 by
Sterling Publishing Company, Inc.
387 Park Avenue South, New York, N.Y. 10016
© 1996 by Helen Nash
Distributed in Canada by Sterling Publishing
% Canadian Manda Group, One Atlantic Avenue, Suite 105
Toronto, Ontario, Canada M6K 3E7
Distributed in Great Britain and Europe by Cassell PLC
Wellington House, 125 Strand, London WC2R 0BB, England
Distributed in Australia by Capricorn Link (Australia) Pty Ltd.
P.O. Box 6651, Baulkham Hills, Business Centre, NSW 2153, Australia
Printed in Hong Kong
All rights reserved

Sterling ISBN 0-8069-4886-8 Trade
0-8069-4283-5 Paper

*For my two children, Michelle and Bill Marocco,
with the wish that their dreams, too, might come true.*

CONTENTS

CONTENTS

INTRODUCTION

Water gardening can be as involved and work-intensive as you like. Often a moment of serendipity is all that happens to lighten the workload. The pond owner with little time or with physical limitations understandably welcomes these moments of insight into labor-saving practices. Sometimes arriving at low-maintenance solutions becomes necessary. Working longer hours, children's summer ball games, or a backache mandates easier methods. My own quest for low-maintenance water gardening was a matter of self-defense. Lower-back pain made it impossible to bend, lift, or toil for any length of time. There has to be an easier way, I said continually. The water gardens, the aquatic plants, the fish—all were too precious for me to give up. I knew I had

to find easier ways to tend them.

What you'll find in this book is the result of that quest. Water gardeners, being warm and kind folks, have shared their moments of discovery with me. You'll find ways to cut short the time required to maintain your water garden. You'll find ways to ease the physical burden of water gardening. Many of the ideas you'll find to be preventive and some you'll find to be labor-lightening. The final result is the same—more time and less pain. So listen to the water, enjoy the lilies, and follow the fish. Water gardening can be more than good for the soul and spirit; it can also be easy on your body and your time limitations. Enjoy!

(opposite page) *Water lilies give color to the low-maintenance garden.* Photo by Greg Speichert.

(left) *Siting a pond within the yard keeps the maintenance level low.* Photo by Steve Koeppel.

(below) *Sawn timbers make an attractive raised pond construction.* Photo by H. Nash.

INTRODUCTION

Terra-cotta containers lining pools catch the eyes of visitors at Denver Botanic Gardens. **Photo courtesy of Joe Tomocik and Denver Botanic Gardens.**

Creative but simple ideas provide beneficial water circulation to the pond. **Photo by Marilyn Ahr.**

Purifying aquatics grow naturally among the stones lining the pond form. **Photo by T.J. Smith**

chapter one

PLANNING &
CONSTRUCTING
FOR LOW
MAINTENANCE

Maintaining a beautiful water garden need not entail much work. **Photo courtesy of Maryland Aquatic Nurseries.**

PLANNING THE WATER FEATURE

A water feature adds magic to the garden—whether a small delight or a focal point of the entire yard. Because the pace of our lives or our health sometimes thwarts diligent maintenance, planning a water feature that incorporates low-impact, low-maintenance may be necessary. The key to low maintenance rests in adopting design and construction methods that prevent future problems.

First of all, make basic decisions about the water feature you want. Do fish swimming about intrigue you? Does the beauty of water lilies reflected in the water refresh you? Does light captured within the sparkling droplets of a fountain enchant you? Does cascading or trickling water captivate you? Does the *sound* of water engender feelings of peace and tranquility in you? Do you crave the lushness and texture of marginal and bog plants to complete your vision? Any of these features can be created so they require minimal maintenance.

The decision of formal or informal pond style involves little more than recognizing the style of your home and the existing landscaping. Formal constructions mandate geometric designs; informal constructions may be free-form and curved. Concrete constructions are more

Waterfalls satisfy both sight and sound. **Photo by H. Nash.**

A pond for koi requires careful planning to provide special conditions for these colorful fish. **Photo by Lee Dreyfuss.**

easily built in formal geometric forms, while curved and free-form designs are more easily constructed with flexible liners.

Also, consider whether you want the feature to be enjoyed from within your home. A water feature sited just outside a window or just off a patio can be both seen and heard. Sited at a distance from the home, a feeling of spaciousness seems to dissolve the physical walls around you.

SITING FOR LOW MAINTENANCE

The usual recommendations for pond-siting befit a low-maintenance pond. Site the pond in an open area of full sun with no trees or nearby shrubs that might deposit leaves in the pond or damage the pond form with root intrusions. Site the pond at a slightly higher elevation of the lay of the land to prevent surface runoff contamination. Site the pond where the water table does not meet the pond's depth, where it might disrupt the liner or crack the molded or concrete form. Unfortunately, not everyone has a gently rolling, fallow cornfield for a backyard. Often a site presents any number of potential maintenance problems. Recognizing and accommodating these potential problems eases the burden of future maintenance.

A pond integrated into the landscaping just off the back deck proves enjoyable from within the house. **Photo by Robert Johnson.**

Siting a pond within the yard keeps the maintenance level low. **Photo by Steve Koeppel.**

The pond sited beneath trees requires planning to prevent additional work created by leaf falls. **Photo by T.J. Smith.**

PREVENTING TREE-RELATED PROBLEMS

Water gardens and fish ponds do not have to be sited in full sun. However, if the amount of sunlight is only two or three hours a day, a very slim selection of water lilies will perform in your pond. On the other hand, there are many other aquatic plants that will grow happily in the shade.

The biggest problem encountered with siting near trees is the collection of leaf debris within the pond. Although leaves collect in ponds in the wild, home water gardens tend to be so much smaller, the decomposition that occurs from accumulated leaves creates problems of water quality and clarity, as well as health problems for the pond's finned inhabitants. Oak and maple leaves and pine needles produce tannic acid, evidenced by the distinctive brown color of the water, in but a few days in the pond. Tannic acid will stress the fish,

Installing pond edging at a slight slope away from the pond, as well as above the surrounding ground level, prevents surface runoff water from entering the pond and creating water-quality problems. **Photo by Oliver Jackson.**

making them more susceptible to parasites and disease; it can also kill them. Leaves that accumulate to any depth invite anaerobic bacteria that produce fish-toxic methane and hydrogen sulfide gases. The fish population is jeopardized, particularly in freezing climates where the pond freezes over, trapping such gases. Prevent such disasters by con-structing a screen over the pond during leaf-fall. (See Chapter 4.)

Root intrusion into the pond membrane creates the need for major repairs. Trenching and severing roots is a major project. Constructing an in-ground con-crete block wall offers a tempor-ary solution, but the roots will still find a way to grow. On such a site a fiberglass membrane or an above-ground construction merits serious consideration.

A recent innovation applicable to such pond situations is Bio-barrier®, produced by Reemay, Inc. in Old Hickory, Tennessee. The product consists of nodules that contain carbon black and trifluralin permanently placed on a nonwoven geotextile fabric. The fabric is installed in a trench

By using soil from the pond excavation, the pond site can easily be elevated enough to prevent runoff into the water garden. **Photo by Joe Cook.**

between the tree and the pond. Roots contacting the two-inch zone around the fabric continue to grow, but are diverted because the division of cells at the root tips is prevented. The nodules release the trifluralin slowly over a long period of time, as long as 15 years.

PREVENTING FUTURE RUNOFF CONTAMINATION

Runoff from the ground surface can create a maintenance nightmare. Lawn fertilizers add significant nutrients to pond water and can make a green pond an overnight occurrence. Likewise, insecticides and herbicides are harmful to both fish and plants. If the site does not have a higher

elevation than the rest of the yard, raise it with spoil from the pond excavation. First strip any sod in long strips of manageable width, roll them, and store in a shady location. Plans to incorporate a paved surrounding area to the pond may require spreading the spoil over the entire area. Mulch, ground covers, or stone can be tapered naturally back into the lay of the yard. Heavy rainfall areas require the pond area to be a good four inches higher than the rest of the yard, while only two inches may be required in dryer climates. Tilting the pond edging slightly down on the outside of the pond edging grants further protection from runoff problems.

PREVENTING HIGH-WATER-TABLE PROBLEMS

A water table that is higher than the depth of the pond causes the liner to bubble up and creates both an aesthetic problem and a dirty pond. Molded ponds and concrete constructions crack and heave from groundwater pressures. Avoid costly repairs by determining the water table in your area before you start construction. Check with your county extension agent or comparable agency or dig a test hole slightly deeper than the projected pond. Observe the water in the hole over the wettest season.

A drainage trench between the pond and the area producing the groundwater, or such a trench fully around the pond, perhaps even under it, directs the groundwater to another area. Constructing such a system involves digging a trench deeper than the deepest pond depth.

The trench deepens at a rate of one inch deeper every 10 feet leading away from the pond area to the designated drainage area. This area may be an existing drainage ditch or a sump area that is excavated and filled with crushed stone. A perforated PVC drainage pipe is placed in the trench and covered with crushed stone. The porous stone filling invites any groundwater at all levels to enter the drainage system. Camouflage the top of the trench with sod replacement, mulch, or groundcover of stone or plants. Prevent clogging by lining the entire trench with geothermal cloth that admits water but prevents soil from working its way in among the stones.

Drainage trenches redirect ground water away from the pond. **Photo by Oliver Jackson.**

If the pond is large enough to require the aid of excavating equipment, use the equipment to help with other chores, too. **Photo by Oliver Jackson.**

MATERIAL SELECTION FOR LOW MAINTENANCE

Materials of good quality and long life prevent recurrent and chronic repairs. Using drop-cloth-quality polyethylene, for example, invites liner degradation and reconstruction in but a year or two. Medium-grade liner materials offer a life expectancy of perhaps 10 years. Top-of-the-line materials, such as thick butyl, or its more common replacement, EPDM PondGard™, offer much longer life expectancies as well as less likelihood of punctures and leaks. Roofing EPDM, while less expensive, may not be fish-safe.

Likewise, preformed or molded pond forms are available in a range of durability. Less expensive plastic forms require careful installation to prevent the pond walls from collapsing and cracking. Especially in areas where the ground and the pond water might freeze, provide two inches or so of sand both beneath the pond and around the walls. If the sand is simply poured in dry, it will settle with rains and create problems. Adding the sand with a slowly running hose washing it down around the pond form will enable it to be compacted. Filling the pond with water as you proceed equalizes pressure between the pond and the ground and prevents the form from be-ing heaved out while work is in progress.

Fiberglass molded pond forms, of course, are the strongest and longest lived. Following the sand padding installation method pre-vents the form from being heaved out by freezing ground.

While a sand layer beneath the preformed pond affords preven-tive maintenance, lined ponds need more protection. Rocks—some sharp—can work their way up through the soil and puncture a liner. Providing an underlay beneath the liner helps prevent these punctures. Thick, felt-like, geothermal fabrics are available for this use. Likewise, a thick layer of newspaper or cardboard may also be used, as may carpet-ing. Avid hobbyist Cliff Tallman advises, however, that if indoor–outdoor carpeting is used, slash it to prevent water from collecting and pushing up the pond liner.

Underlay fabrics are an easy way to provide liner protection from rocks working their way up through the soil. **Photo by Oliver Jackson.**

EPDM liners are flexible and easy to fit into free-form excavations. **Photo by Oliver Jackson.**

Long-lived fiberglass constructions are available in sections that allow more creativity in designing preformed ponds. **Photo by Robert Johnson.**

PLANNING & CONSTRUCTING FOR LOW MAINTENANCE

Even very small preformed pond shells make delightful water gardens. **Photo by Oliver Jackson.**

LEVELING
THE POND

A pond that is not perfectly level around its upper edge presents more than an irritatingly lopsided appearance. The pond may flood easily, creating problems in the surrounding area. The portion of the pond wall exposed to sunlight may experience degradation from UV sunlight rays. If the liner is a bonded material, this results in a release of the bonding with holes occurring in the liner. Other liners, including plastic preformed ponds, may become brittle and crack. Hence, it is especially important that the upper edge of the pond is level all the way around. Carpenter's spirit levels, available in several lengths, determine the perfect level from one point to another. A clear hose filled with water compares the water level from one end of the hose to the other as measured against stakes pounded in around the pond perimeter.

A laser level needs only one person to operate it and ensures that the pond edges are perfectly level. **Photo by Oliver Jackson.**

Carpenter's spirit levels, available in a variety of sizes, check whether construction is level. **Photo courtesy of Maryland Aquatic Nurseries.**

VERTICAL WALLS AND PLANTING SHELVES FOR LOW MAINTENANCE

While there is more than one way to build a pond, constructing for low maintenance demands one priority—accessibility. There are times you must go into the pond. Sloped sides make this hazardous—slippery algae coatings are part of nature even if wet pond-lining materials are not slick. Carrying a bucket of fish or a dripping pot of lilies up a slippery slope invites a fall. Constructing nearly vertical walls makes for safer motion, as do reasonably spaced steps. A one-foot spacing, for example, is not difficult to navigate and actually benefits the pond, since many marginal aquatics and dwarf or pygmy lilies will grow happily in one foot of water.

Still another factor is safety. If the step is created wide enough all around the pond, tragedies resulting from accidental tumbles into the pond, especially by toddlers, may be prevented. Seren-

Keeping the side walls nearly vertical makes it easier to enter and leave the pond. **Photo by Oliver Jackson.**

PLANNING & CONSTRUCTING FOR LOW MAINTENANCE

dipitous benefits include added foraging area for fish among marginal aquatics on the shelf and the predator barrier the aquatics create.

Products such as Lineups™ facilitate vertical wall construction while lending additional support to the side walls. **Photo by Oliver Jackson.**

Providing a slightly lower area in the pond edging allows for controlled rain overflows. Sloping the bottom to a deeper point allows easy drainage with a submerged pump. **Photo by Oliver Jackson.**

PROVIDING FOR EASY POND DRAINAGE

A pond kept reasonably clean does not require draining and cleaning for several years. However, should a water-quality problem make it necessary to fully drain the pond, planned construction minimizes the task. Often, molded ponds, especially fiberglass, come with a sump well in them. Provide such an area in a lined pond by sloping the entire bottom to one deepest point.

Even with a sump hole in the pond, a small bit of water may remain once the recycling pump is removed. Sopping up this water with towels and wringing them into a bucket can be back-breaking work. A simple wet-dry shop vac easily completes the operation.

LOW-MAINTENANCE POND EDGINGS

Stacking flat stones around the edge is the easiest way to finish off a pond. But in the long run, loose stones involve greater maintenance. They can fall into the pond, possibly tearing the liner. They can result in accidental falls, perhaps into the pond. And they present havens for

Concrete may stabilize edge stones and may also prevent weeds from growing in between. **Photo by Oliver Jackson.**

Paving blocks or bricks also create a low-maintenance pond edge. Prepare properly, layer with sand, and set the stonework firmly into the surrounding ground.

Large edging stones need adequate anchoring to prevent them from tumbling into the pond when it becomes necessary to stand on them. **Photo by Karla Anderson.**

blowing seeds that sprout into unsightly weeds.

Low-maintenance edging involves stabilizing the edging material within mortar or reinforced concrete or using sufficiently large, heavy stones that will remain securely in place.

Most pond-construction guides suggest bringing the pond liner below the edging stone and then back up behind it. However, for weed prevention, extend the liner a foot beyond the pond perimeter. Rocks or stonework at the pond edge can be secured to the liner with spray polyfoam. Place stone or mulch on the extended pond liner to provide a weed-free perimeter.

Extend the liner out a distance from the pond edge to provide a weed barrier immediately around the pond. **Photo by Oliver Jackson.**

Cover the extended liner with mulch for camouflage. Potted plants can seasonally vary the landscape edging. **Photo by Oliver Jackson.**

"Oly Ola"™ landscape edging is another material that can provide a vertical pond edge. **Photo courtesy of Maryland Aquatic Nurseries.**

PLANNING & CONSTRUCTING FOR LOW MAINTENANCE

Bringing the surrounding paving up to the pond edge avoids weed control later on. **Photo by Cla Allgood.**

Installing the pond within a deck is another way to avoid edge maintenance. **Photo by Greg Maxwell.**

ACCESSIBILITY OF SERVICES

Having to haul 100 feet of hose from the nearest spigot is not low maintenance. Long extension cords lying on the ground present many potential problems. An electrical short from a wet outlet can burn up the pump or electrocute the fish; the accidental disconnection of electricity running a bio-filter can kill bacteria and cause critical water-quality problems. Any services employed must be close enough

Safety features, such as this covered electrical box, prevent maintenance problems. **Photo by Oliver Jackson.**

RAISED POND CONSTRUCTIONS FOR LOW MAINTENANCE

In warmer climates, build raised ponds of landscape or sawn timbers for low maintenance. Construct the pond edges to form benches for easy access to the plants within. A raised pond can be built to any height for the owner's needs—wheelchair height, for example.

A variation of the raised pond—concrete-block pedestals supporting a strong box, a liner set within it, and a smooth edging around the top—creates a "desktop" pond. Such construction accommodates marginal aquatics and dwarf, pygmy, or tropical water lilies.

to the pond for their safe and convenient use.

With a double-spigot attachment affixed to the outside water outlet, the pond hose can be buried in a more accessible storage site. Bury electrical cables properly, connect them through a ground-fault circuit interrupter, and provide waterproof housings.

A different option for the naturally balanced pond that does not involve a recycling pump is to use solar-powered lights around the pond area. Placing these lights into nonsubmerged pots of soil within the pond provides in-pond lighting without the hassle of electrical maintenance.

Sawn timbers make an attractive raised pond construction. **Photo by H. Nash.**

Very small tabletop ponds afford easy maintenance. **Photo by Betsy Sakata.**

A Mexican soapstone fountain is converted into an accessible water garden. **Photo by M.J. Girot.**

Stones embedded into concrete combine with mulching for low maintenance. **Photo by Cliff Tallman.**

LOW-MAINTENANCE WATER GARDENS

chapter two

LOW-MAINTENANCE FILTRATION & WATER QUALITY

Water hyacinth (Eichhornia *spp.) removes nutrients from the water to aid in natural filtration.* **Photo by H. Nash.**

The topic of filtration creates controversy among water gardeners. In fact, it may not be necessary. Depending upon the situation, any of three types of filtration may be used to maintain the pond at a healthy state: natural filtration, particulate filtration, and bio-filtration. While each form may be complicated, low maintenance requires fairly simple systems.

NATURAL FILTRATION

Natural filtration simply uses plants to perform the filtering functions within the pond. Usually this refers to the biological process of using up excess nutrients, phosphates, and minerals in the water to prevent lower-order algae plant forms from accessing them. The most basic form of natural filtration merely provides the appropriate amount of higher-order plants to keep the water clear. The plants most often used for this function are the submerged aquatics, often called oxygenators or clarifiers.

The basic formula of how many submerged plants are required in a pond is one bunch (of five to six plants per bunch) for every one to two square feet (0.1 to 0.2 sq. m) of water surface. If the pond is stocked heavily with

Pea gravel lining planted directly with submerged aquatics keeps the pond water crystal-clear. Photo by Ronald E. Everhart.

Parrot's feather (Myriophyllum aquatica), while not as efficient as other submerged aquatics, will provide some nutrient removal in natural filtration. Photo by Ronald E. Everhart.

A separate, smaller pond planted with aquatics provides natural filtration. **Photo by Carol Christensen.**

fish, perhaps even more will be required.

Plants selected for nutrient removal should be suited to the geographical area of the pond. Cold-water submerged plants such as *elodea canadensis*, for example, will not grow as well in the much warmer waters of a tropical pond. By the same token, tropical submerged plants will not survive the winter in colder climates.

Similarly, water gardeners report effective control of algae-producing nutrients by growing the tropical water hyacinth *(Eichhornia)* or water lettuce *(Pistia)* in the pond.

RICHARD SCHUCK'S 10% SOLUTION

Maryland Aquatic Nurseries' owner Richard Schuck devised what he called "The 10% Solution" some years ago. This system uses a plant basin equal in size to 10 percent of the pond area. The basin is filled with aquatic plants, and the pond water is recycled through it once every two to four hours. The plants not only remove excess nutrients that feed green-water algae, they also settle and filter out particulate solid waste matter.

Whatever its size, the filter should be 12 to 18 inches (30 to 46 cm) deep and equipped with an overflow so that it can act as a settling chamber for solid wastes. Pond water enters the unit at the furthest point from the pond to maximize the water flow distance for settling activity. Mr. Schuck notes that a narrow filter is more efficient than a round-shaped unit.

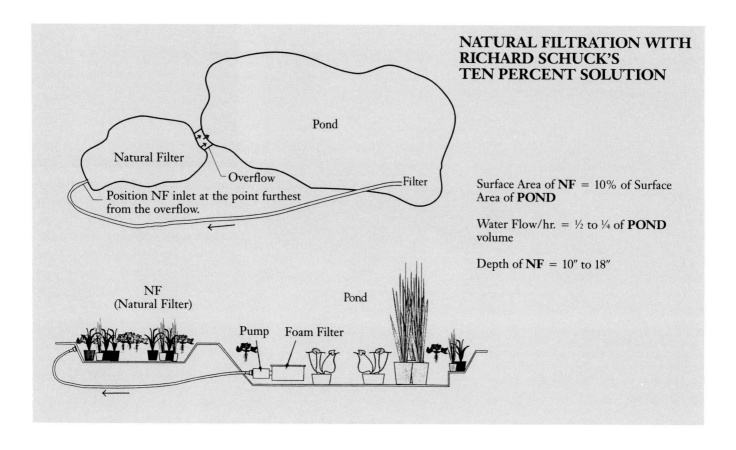

NATURAL FILTRATION WITH RICHARD SCHUCK'S TEN PERCENT SOLUTION

Pond

Natural Filter

Overflow

Filter

Position NF inlet at the point furthest from the overflow.

NF (Natural Filter)

Pond

Pump

Foam Filter

Surface Area of **NF** = 10% of Surface Area of **POND**

Water Flow/hr. = ½ to ¼ of **POND** volume

Depth of **NF** = 10″ to 18″

Water irises work well in a natural filter. **Photo by Greg Speichert.**

Plant suggestions for the filter unit include water hyacinth *(Eichhornia)*, water lettuce *(Pistia* sp.)*, water mint *(Mentha aquatica)*, watercress *(Nasturtium officinale)*, water iris *(Iris pseudacorus, Iris versicolor, Iris laevagata)*, cattails *(Typha* ssp.)*, arrowhead *(Saggitaria* ssp.)*, papyrus, and umbrella palm *(Cyperus* ssp.)*.

Besides removing excess nutrients from the water and preventing green water, this system is truly low-maintenance. Normal plant care is observed but, with the plants collected together in one out-of-pond area, both time and labor are minimized.

Watercress, a lover of moving water, is a perfect plant to aid in water-clarifying in streams and waterfalls. **Photo by Ronald E. Everhart.**

LOW-MAINTENANCE FILTRATION & WATER QUALITY

SUBMERGED PUMP MAINTENANCE

Standard pump maintenance requires that the pump be removed from the pond as necessary to clean off and dispose of any collected debris that might slow the pump, stress it, or cause it to burn out. Since most pumps come with only a small filter screen, it may be necessary to take care of this as often as several times a week in the early spring or fall and once a week throughout the summer. Remove the pump from the pond and hose the filter screen clean. If you don't wish to clean the pump so frequently, the filter screen area should be increased. Attach a larger filter box to the pump or increase the particle screening area by wrapping fiberglass screening or heavy-duty foam around the pump and set it in an open-weave plastic basket. The larger the surface area of the filter screen, the less often the pump will need to be cleaned.

Another way to lessen pump maintenance is to set the pump about 6 inches (15 cm) from the bottom of the pond. This keeps the pump from pulling settled particle matter from the pond bottom.

The cattail family (Typha spp.) offers many sizes of plants to aid in natural nutrient removal. **Photo by Ronald E. Everhart.**

Recirculating water pumps come in a variety of sizes to fit any water garden. **Photo courtesy of Little Giant Pump Corporation.**

Filter wool/fabric wrapped around a pump placed in a basket with handles makes for accessible maintenance. **Photo by Oliver Jackson.**

Pumps may be purchased with attached filter boxes that aid in cleaning the water. **Photo courtesy of Supreme Pump Manufacturers.**

JOE B. DEKKER'S SURFACE SKIMMER

Many years ago, Joe B. Dekker, a pond designer and builder in New Jersey, developed a surface skimmer filtration system based on the skimmer filter systems used in swimming pools. The system can be homemade relatively inexpensively. It effectively moves surface debris into the skimmer bag, where it is easily emptied as needed. The result is a clean pond unhampered by accumulating debris on the pond bottom.

Filter media, commonly called foam, is available in different densities and thicknesses. **Photo by Oliver Jackson.**

The system consists of a 30-gallon plastic trash can installed immediately adjacent to the pond with the opening of the unit sealed to the pond liner. A submerged pump in the bottom of the can pulls in the surface water and returns it to the pond through a flexible hose routed to a waterfall on another side of the pond. A nylon laundry bag hung on hooks inside the can collects the debris. The can lid is camou-flaged with spray polyfoam and rocks and sand or by a flat stone. A natural or bio-filter can be included and set up at the waterfall.

CONSTRUCTION

Materials Needed

one 30-gallon (120 l), heavy-duty, plastic trash can

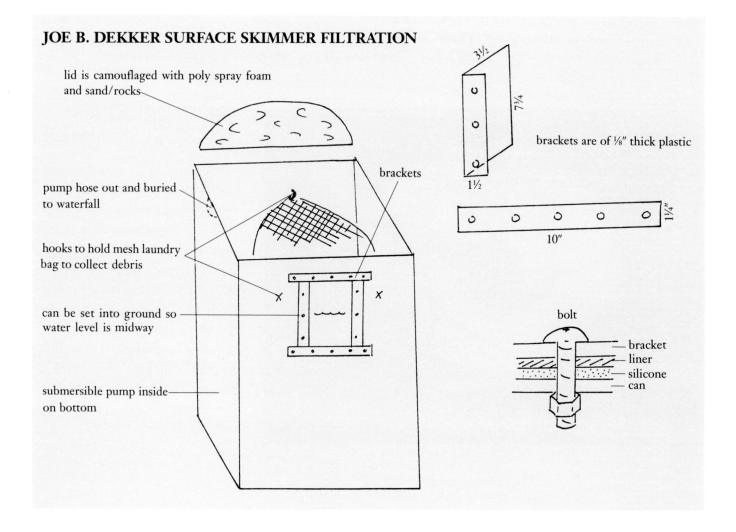

JOE B. DEKKER SURFACE SKIMMER FILTRATION

lid is camouflaged with poly spray foam and sand/rocks

pump hose out and buried to waterfall

hooks to hold mesh laundry bag to collect debris

can be set into ground so water level is midway

submersible pump inside on bottom

brackets

brackets are of ⅛" thick plastic

3½

7¾

1½

10"

1¼"

bolt

bracket
liner
silicone
can

one piece of ⅛″ (0.3 cm) thick plastic at least 10 × 9″ (25 × 23 cm), which will be cut into pieces, one measuring 10 × 1½″ (25 × 4 cm) and two measuring 7 × 1½″ (18 × 4 cm)

eleven ⁵⁄₃₂–1¼″ (0.04–3 cm) bolts with nuts

five screw-in hooks

one tube of RTV single-component silicone

one nylon-mesh laundry bag

1¼″ (3 cm) flexible black hosing to reach from pump to waterfall

submersible water garden pump of at least 750 GPH

hose adapter, if required, to affix hose to pump

Optional: filter foam to fit inside dimension of trash can

spray polyfoam for camouflaging lid

Preliminaries

1. Excavate a hole adjacent to the pond edge to accommodate a 30-gallon (100 l), heavy-duty, plastic trash can so the water level of the pond will be at the midpoint of the centered 7 × 8″ (18–20 cm) cut-out 1½″ (4 cm) from the top of the can.
2. Layer the bottom of the excavation with 2–4 inches (5–10 cm) of well-tamped crushed stone.
3. Provide a shallow trench from the can to the waterfall for routing the flexible return hose.

Preparing the Can

1. Mark and cut out an 8 × 7″ (20 × 18 cm) rectangle 1½″ (4 cm) down from the top and centered on the front of the can.
2. Cut a slot from the side of the top for the pump hose and electrical cord to exit the can when the lid is replaced.
3. Cut three brackets from ⅛″ (0.3 cm) thick plastic:
   Cut one at 10 × 1¼″ (25.5 × 3 cm) (for the horizontal bottom edge of hole)
   Cut two at 7 × 1¼″ (18 × 3 cm) (for the left and right vertical edges)
4. Match up brackets to the opening edges of the can and drill holes for bolts.
5. Set the can into the prepared excavation.
6. Apply ¼″ (0.6 cm) thick by ½″ (1.3 cm) wide RTV single-component silicone compound around the face of the cut-out of the can. Press liner to the face of the can and hold it firmly to the silicone by bolting on the three brackets.
7. Use the cut-out of the can as a guide to cut the liner across the top and down the sides for a matching hole. Fold the liner flap to the inside of the can.
8. Attach two screw-in hooks approximately 8″ (20 cm) down from the top of the can on each side of the cut-out and two screw-in hooks 1″ (2.5 cm) down from the top on each side of the cut-out so the pond liner flap is enclosed within the bag. Attach another hook 1″ (2.5 cm) down from the top to the center of the opposite side of the can. (The skimmer bag will hang on these five hooks.)
9. Connect the flexible hosing to the pump and place the pump in the bottom of the can. Route the hose and the pump's electrical cord from the can.
10. Optional foam may be cut to fit over the pump for additional small-particle filtration.
11. Attach the edge of a nylon laundry bag onto the hooks inside the can while keeping slack at a minimum.
12. Poly foam may be sprayed onto the can lid. While it is wet, sand and small gravel may be tossed onto it for camouflage. Flat paving stones can also be used to hide the lid.

Using the System

1. During operation, the water level should be maintained at one-half to two-thirds of the way up the opening of the cut-out.
2. Clean out the nylon bag as needed. Likewise, hose clean any foam media as needed.

BIO-FILTERS

Because low-maintenance water gardening assumes that the number of fish kept in the pond is at a minimum, bio-filtration is not usually necessary. However, ponds supplied with water containing chloramines may find a bio-filter unit of benefit to counter the extra ammonia added to the water to create the long-lived chloramines. Bio-filtration is based upon the the work of nitrifying bacteria that convert ammonia to nitrite and then to nitrates. It is not used to keep the water clear unless natural plant filtration is used as well. There are many manufactured bio-filters available in the marketplace, some of which may be low-maintenance. If you do not want to construct your own filter system, compare the designs of manufactured products with the proven homemade varieties discussed in this chapter.

Constructing a homemade bio-filter similar to the one purchased permits double filtration. **Photo by Oliver Jackson.**

NITRIFYING BACTERIA

All bio-filters use nitrifying bacteria. Although these bacteria will naturally enter the pond's ecosystem, waiting for this to happen may take half the season. The time frame can be shortened

Nitrifying bacteria may be added to the bio-filter or, in some cases, directly to the pond water. **Photo courtesy of Aquarium Pharmaceuticals.**

by "seeding" the bio-filter with a prepared commercial mix. These preparations are available in two forms, liquid and dried. Liquid forms may have a shelf life of only two to four weeks. If the packaging date is not labeled, it is not possible to know if it is a viable population. Dried forms are packaged with enzymes and must be dissolved in water before being introduced to the pond. If properly stored, these formulations may have a shelf life of a year or more. The maximum efficiency of nitrifying bacteria is limited to water temperatures above 55°F (13°C) and pH ranges between 6.5 and 7.8.

Bio-filters used in areas where the winter temperatures drop below 55°F (12°C) must be removed, cleaned, and stored for the winter. They can be restarted and reseeded in the spring when the temperatures return above 55°F (13°C). Generally, the water flows through the filter at a rate

A whiskey barrel creates a decorative bio-filter. **Photo by Cliff Tallman.**

of one to two gallons (4–7.5 l) per minute per square foot (sq. m) of filter surface. (To determine an approximate bio-filter size for your pond, divide the pond's volume in gallons (litres) by 125 (5000) to determine the amount of media surface required in sq. ft. (in sq. m). Multiply the square footage (metrage) of media surface by one and two (40 and 80) and then each by 60 minutes to determine the range in pump size for the necessary flow rate. If the pond contains less than 2500 gallons (9500 l), the water should be run through the filter once every two hours; ponds of over 2500 gallons (9500 l) may halve that rate. The hose should be at least ¾" (2 cm) in diameter.

Bio-filter setups can be very complicated and demand considerable maintenance. For our low-maintenance purposes, we'll look at bio-filter designs that are easily constructed and easily tended.

THE HENRY REIMER BIO-FILTER

Easy to make and easy to use characterize this simple bio-filter design. Although the filter unit itself is sited outside the pond, the pump is submerged within the pond. The system will effectively treat a 1,000 gallon pond with a reasonable fish population and careful feeding practices.

CONSTRUCTION
Materials Needed

200–500 GPH submersible pump

hose adapter to ½ inch, if necessary

one half of a 45-gallon drum or barrel

lining material, if necessary

cutting tool for drum

1½ inch (4 cm) diameter white PVC pipe of sufficient length for return provisions

aquarium silicone or single-component RTV silicone

polyethylene pipe in pieces 1 inch (2.5 cm) diameter × 2 inches (5 cm) long, to fill ¾ full in drum

cover for drum or barrel top

½ inch (1.3 cm) hose connecting from pump to filter barrel outside pond

1. Set up the pump within the pond. A filter screen on the pump's intake prevents debris from cycling through the pump. The ½ inch (1.3 cm) diameter hose is affixed to the pump, using an adapter if necessary. Direct the hose to the out-of-pond filter location. (This may be at the back of the waterfall.)
2. Cut out a 1½ inch (4 cm) diameter hole near the top of the drum or barrel to accommodate the PVC outlet pipe.
3. Be sure the PVC outlet pipe is long enough to return water to the pond in the desired channel, whether directly or via the waterfall.
4. Seal the PVC outlet pipe into the container hole. Use a thin bead of the silicone sealer and allow it to cure for 24 hours before exposing it to water.
5. Fill the drum to just below the PVC pipe with the polyethylene pipe. Predator netting may be substituted for the pipe pieces.
6. Direct the hose leading from the pump into the bottom of the barrel. (Water recycles up through the media and out the PVC pipe into the courseway.)
7. Start the pump and add seed bacteria according to directions.

HENRY REIMER BIO-FILTER

PVC return pipe via waterfall

PVC pipe sections

water enters at bottom

bury hose outside pond

water return hose

pump in pond

RUNNING AND MAINTAINING

The pump should be run 24 hours a day during periods of temperatures consistently above 50°F (10°C). No maintenance is required during this period. In the autumn or winter, when the temperatures stabilize below 50°F (10°C), remove the hose from the drum and set up the pump for winter use, if desired. Clean out the filter drum and store for the winter.

A bio-filter helps keep water clear of green-water algae. **Photo courtesy of Little Giant Pump Corporation.**

The Kerns bio-filter is a simple way to have clear water of good quality. **Photo by Mary Kerns.**

THE MARY KERNS BIO-FILTER

Mary and Bob Kerns have been raising and breeding koi in both indoor and outdoor ponds for over 25 years. The bio-filter they use produces clear, untainted water even with heavy fish loads. Unique to their design, the filter is submerged within the pond.

Materials Needed

rectangular heavy-duty plastic storage box, large enough to contain the pump and media with room to spare

enough lava rock pieces to fill the container to within a few inches of the top

flexible black hose, extending from the pump to the top of the waterfall

hose adapters, if necessary, to attach hose to the pump

an electric or battery-operated drill

nitrifying bacteria

Making the Bio-filter

1. Rinse the lava rocks well to prevent their dust from coloring the pond water.
2. Mark the container lid with a hole the size needed to bring the outlet hose out of the box. A drill may be used to remove this section. Be sure the hose will fit through.

3. Use the largest drill bit to make holes a quarter to half inch (0.6–1.3 cm) apart over the entire lid.
4. Set the pump with its connected hose in the bottom of the container and fill lava rock all around it and up to within a few inches (5 cm) of the top.
5. Thread the outlet hose through the lid and lower the lid so it can be fastened securely once the bacteria have been poured in.
6. Set the filter in the pond in the desired location, pour in bacteria, and fasten the lid.
7. Bury the outlet hose up to the point of water re-entry if a waterfall setup is used. If a fountain is set up, the hose should be connected to it.

Mark the top of the plastic storage unit for the pump hose and cord to access the filter. **Photo by H. Nash.**

Thread the lid onto the hose that is affixed to the pump inside the container. **Photo by H. Nash.**

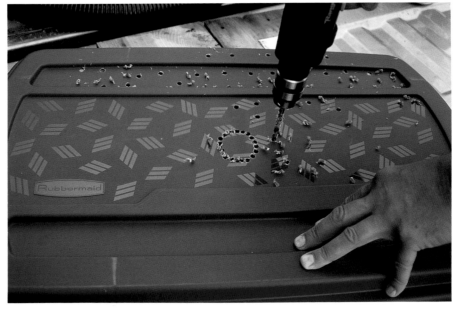

Drill holes in the top of the container so water can enter the unit. **Photo by H. Nash.**

Fill around and over the pump with washed lava rock. **Photo by H. Nash.**

LOW-MAINTENANCE FILTRATION & WATER QUALITY

Replace the lid and submerge filter box in pond. **Photo by H. Nash.**

RUNNING AND MAINTAINING

The pump should be run around the clock in order to assure the nitrifying bacteria the oxygen they need to live. No maintenance is required during the season. When the temperatures stabilize below 50°F (10°C) in the autumn or winter, remove the pump from the pond. Set up the pump for winter operation, if desired, and store the cleaned filter until spring.

THE DEAN EVANS BIO-FILTER

Indoor water gardening hobbyist Dean Evans has devised a simple out-of-pond bio-filter that he uses with his $4 \times 8 \times 3'$ deep ($1.2 \times 2.4 \times 1$ m) landscape-timber, above-ground pond. The pond holds approximately 350 gallons (1300 l) of water and is maintained throughout the year in a Florida sunroom.

Materials Needed

white PVC 1½ inch (4 cm) diameter pipe equal to diameter and height of the can

2 PVC elbow fittings

2 PVC spacers to fit in bottom half of can

1 plastic or fiberglass drip plate to fit inside can diameter

1 egg crate drip plate to fit inside can diameter

28 pounds lava rock, well rinsed

sixteen 12-inch (30 cm) brushes, tie-wrapped to plastic-coated or PVC bar

4 rubber straps

1 thick, heavy-grade filter foam piece cut to inner can diameter

one 30-gallon (120 l) plastic trash can with lid

one RIO 2100 submersible pump or equivalent to produce 486 GPH at 3' (90 cm) head

single-component RTV silicone

drill

fittings for attaching pump hosings

A lanai fish pond benefits from the use of a bio-filter. **Photo by Dean Evans.**

CONSTRUCTION

1. Drill holes into the spray bar section of PVC piping, plug ends and affix inlet PVC pipe with silicone. Allow it to cure 24 hours before using. (Attach fitting for pump hosing intake.)

2. Cut a hole in the can lid for the spray bar pipe fixture.

3. Cut a piece of PVC pipe to half the diameter of the can. Cut another to three-quarters of the height of the can. Join with elbow joint.

4. Set the elbow joint on the bottom of the can and mark the side for the outlet piping hole. Cut a hole for the outlet pipe egress.

5. Affix a long enough piece of PVC to the outlet with the elbow joint and fit through the cut-out. (Attach the fitting to accommodate hose fitting to outlet.)

6. Set PVC spacers in the bottom of the can.

7. Place the grate over the spacers and the elbow-jointed return piping.

8. Place the lava rock on the grate.

9. Tie-wrap the brushes in a row to the bar and affix the bar to the top of the elbow bend of exiting PVC pipe in the side of the can. (There will be a space between the brushes and the lava rock below.)

10. Fit an egg crate drip plate over the brushes. Attach it to the top edge of the can with rubber straps.

11. Cut and fit the filter mat to the inside can diameter and place it over the egg crate drip plate.

12. Fix the lid over the can and set it up outside the pond.

13. Attach the hose from the pump to the entry in the top of the can. Be sure the side outlet is set to return water to the pond.

14. Set the pump in the bottom of the pond and start it up.

15. Add seed bacteria to the running filter.

RUNNING AND MAINTENANCE

Although Dean Evans has gone as long as 2½ months without a water exchange, he usually performs a partial water change in the pond once a month. The filter mat must be rinsed once a month, sometimes more often. Since Evans' pond is located in a Florida sunroom, he keeps the filter running year-round. He cleans it out and restarts it once a year.

The lanai pond is constructed of landscape timbers and lined with a flexible membrane. **Photo by Dean Evans.**

The filter canister is set on a ledge at the rear of the pond to allow the water to return. **Photo by Dean Evans.**

OTHER LOW-MAINTENANCE BIO-FILTER TIPS

Because lava rock and other filter media may clog with particulate matter, West Coast hobbyist Ron Williams has devised a way of keeping it clear. He uses a ½" (1.3 cm) PVC pipe run to the bottom of his rock filter, where the pipe is hooked into a horizontal ring full of ⅛" (0.3 cm) holes. When his filter shows signs of slowing, he turns off his pump, plugs up the outflow pipe from the filter, and attaches a wet-dry vacuum to an adapter on the top inflow pipe. The air blown into the pipe bubbles up through the rock media and dislodges debris that floats to the top, where it is skimmed off.

Koi keepers Joe and Sherri White share another low-maintenance tip about filter media. They've discovered Bio-Fill™, PVC shavings called bio-ribbon that easily flush clean and offer about 250 square feet (750 sq. m) of media surface per cubic foot (cu. m). But one cubic foot will support approximately 80 pounds (100 k) of fish.

Pond Care owner Bob Johnson, of Fresno, notes that using

George Rosicky's Leisure Bio Filter design features centrifugal pipes below the filter mats. **Photo by H. Nash.**

wood within a filter may leach harmful acids into the water, as well as color it. The only wood he recommends is cedar. Bob uses PVC piping for his filter constructions. He notes that white PVC pipe is for potable water and is fish-safe, while the gray PVC contains UV inhibitors and is not certified potable.

And, in the Midwest, Cliff Tallman notes that air conditioner filters are inexpensive and easy to clean. Do remember that the finer the filtration media, the quicker it will clog and the harder it is to clean.

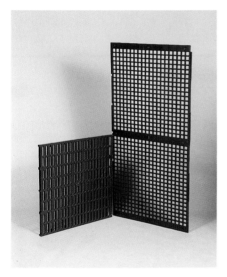

Filter grates are available from most pond suppliers. **Photo courtesy of Maryland Aquatic Nurseries.**

Lava rock piled around the submerged pump in a bucket may be sufficient in small ponds. **Photo by T.J. Smith.**

A UV sterilizer, encased within a quartz sleeve and set to treat water before it enters the bio-filter, may help control free-floating green water algae. **Photo by Oliver Jackson.**

UV STERILIZERS

UV sterilizers are most commonly associated with aquariums or koi-keeping. However, they can offer a relatively low-maintenance method of clear-water control in the water garden, too. A UV sterilizer will *not* affect the water's chemistry, lower a fish's immune system, clean the pond of dead and decaying matter, or harm an established bio-filter. A UV sterilizer *will* kill waterborne algae, viruses, fungi, and protozoa. Naturally, any sediment created by the UV's actions should be vacuumed from the pond.

As an electrical device, the UV sterilizer must be certified as weatherproof and will bear such a label. The device used in a pond must be considerably stronger than those sold for aquarium use. A lamp rated at 30,000 microwatt sec./cm^2 will tend most good-sized backyard ponds. Smaller units are available for smaller ponds. The pond water should pass through the unit at least once every six hours, optimally at a turnover rate of once every two hours. The lamp should be housed within a quartz sleeve to protect the lamp from cold pond water and to allow it to attain full power.

Maintenance is quite simple: replace the bulb once a season.

Never look directly at the UV lightbulb when it is turned on. **Photo by Oliver Jackson.**

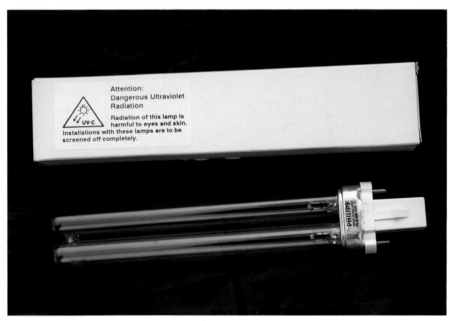

UV lightbulbs should be replaced each year. **Photo by Oliver Jackson.**

LOW-MAINTENANCE FILTRATION & WATER QUALITY

Incorporating a bog garden within the pond provides natural filtration. **Photo by Greg Speichert.**

Waterfall effects need not be on a grand scale. **Photo by T.J. Smith**

Decorative tub gardens offer a low-maintenance water-garden option. **Photo courtesy of Maryland Aquatic Nurseries.**

LOW-MAINTENANCE FILTRATION & WATER QUALITY

chapter three

LOW-MAINTENANCE PLANT & FISH CARE

LOW-MAINTENANCE AND AQUATIC PLANTS

Water gardening presents a unique gardening situation. Unlike normal gardening, where plants may or may not receive ideal growing conditions and therefore may or may not achieve maximum growth, water gardening is an all-or-nothing experience. If there's water in the pond, aquatic plants will usually grow well. Consequently, we are dealing with actively growing plants throughout the season. Repotting aquatics is an expected seasonal activity. Neglecting that chore results in plants jumping out of their pots, escaping the pots through holes, or literally pushing out the pot walls to create unwieldy, massive root masses. For people with bad backs or little time, this one

The Lotus **Roseum plenum** *may be cared for more easily in its own pot than within the pond itself.* **Photo courtesy of Maryland Aquatic Nurseries.**

A water lily showing several growth points within a pot needs to be divided and repotted. **Photo by Ronald E. Everhart.**

chore is the most desirable to convert into low-maintenance proportions. Wet soil is heavy. Pea gravel topping used with the plants adds even more weight. Large pots of wet soil with pea gravel topping and a vigorously growing plant can produce living nightmares of repotting.

POT SELECTION

Most water garden books suggest using pots with holes in the bottom or even mesh baskets for planting aquatics. The logic is valid. Vigorously growing plants need room for their roots to seek further nourishment. Yet, these extending roots often create part of the maintenance problem. Do these plants really need holes in the pots? As a commercial grower, Steve Stroupe of Davis Creek Nurseries has had to deal pragmatically with the question. His findings have been corroborated by others in the industry, as well as by home hobbyists. Most aquatic plants do not seem to suffer from being grown in hole-less pots.

Attempting to ease some of the workload, Steve made still another discovery: aquatic plants do not usually require as much soil as is traditionally suggested. Kelly Billings of Maryland Aquatic Nurseries explains it simply, that in nature, aquatic plants are typically surface-growing plants. They don't send down long taproots like many non-aquatic plants. If we look at how the plants typically grow, it is only logical that the pots we use for aquatics offer greater surface area rather than greater depth.

This is good news for low-maintenance water gardeners—less hassle with root masses and less weight with the potted plants. Pots, then, to use for aquatic plants are wide-mouthed, holeless mum pots, shallow plastic oil pans, or small dish pans.

PLANT SELECTION FOR LOW MAINTENANCE

Regardless of easier potting techniques, some aquatic plants are such vigorous growers that nothing will prevent their leaps from

A shallow, wide dishpan offers longer growing time for many aquatic plants. **Photo by Oliver Jackson.**

Aggressive plants such as floating heart (Nymphoides *spp.) can create maintenance problems.* **Photo by Oliver Jackson.**

Pennywort (Hydrocotyle *sp.) needs constant monitoring to control rampant growth.* **Photo by Greg Speichert.**

pots and taking over the pond. Plants that spread by runners, such as water clovers (*Marsilea* spp.), floating heart (*Nymphoides* spp.), and pennyworts (*Hydrocotle* spp.), are obvious examples. These plants are easily controlled if you have the time to religiously cut them back as they begin their ramblings. However, in the true spirit of low maintenance, these plants need to be avoided.

Plants that reseed prolifically should also be avoided. The

*Variegated cattail (*Typha latifolia variegatus*) proves to be less rampant in growth in comparison to other family members.* **Photo by Ronald E. Everhart.**

most obvious plant of this type is water plantain (*Alisma plantago* sp.) A lovely, informal plant, it crops up in any pot with soil and quickly takes over slower-growing plants. Many aquatic plantsmen consider the plant a weed. Smaller forms of the *eleocharis* family, such as spike rush, have a similar, if less visually obtrusive, habit.

Likewise, plants of great vigor that are likely to jump the pot, or push out the pot side, are wise to avoid for low maintenance. Most cattails (*Typha* sp.) are in this category. However, the variegated form seems to be a slower propa-

Bulrush (Scirpus spp.) *has a more compact root growth that is easier to control.* **Photo by Ronald E. Everhart.**

Pickerel plants (Pontederia cordata) *require wide-mouthed pots to accommodate more than one year's growth.* **Photo by Ronald E. Everhart.**

gator that is happy for a couple of seasons in the same wide-mouthed pot. Likewise, the micro-miniature cattail, *Typha* 'Europa', can be contained for a year or two within the same pot.

In a similar vein, some aquatics, such as pickerel (*Pontederia* sp.), grow from substantial rootstock that is left behind the following year as the new growth extends outward from it. Often the second year in the same pot finds a huge mass of dead root in the pot's center and new plants growing at the pot's edge or from outside the pot. Bullrushes (*Scirpus* sp.) also tend to send out fresh growth around the dead center growth. However, they tend to be more clump-growing and, therefore, more easily confined to the same pot for a longer period of time than the pickerel weeds.

LOWER-MAINTENANCE AQUATIC PLANTS

Variegated sweet flag, Acorus calamus variegatus, *provides light and life to the pond. Growing in fans from an elongated surface rhizome, the plant tends to travel across the pot with side shoots developing into their own branches. A shallow, wide-mouthed pot provides growing room for more than one season.* Photo by Greg Speichert.

Acorus gramineus 'Ogon' *is a semi-hardy dwarf form of sweet flag. Its growth habit forms fans from the growing root that makes its way shallowly across the pot. Pot this plant in a shallow, wide-mouthed pot.* **Photo courtesy of Maryland Aquatic Nurseries.**

Arrow arum, **Peltandra** *spp., is among the slower-growing aquatic perennials. Be sure to feed the plant regularly when it is left in the same soil for more than one year.* **Photo by Greg Speichert.**

Phyla lanceolata, *frog fruit, is a low-growing, hardy aquatic that can be easily controlled by trimming back its scrambling growth. It offers enchanting blooms through the summer months. Keep it in a wide-mouthed pot in shallow water.* **Photo by Greg Speichert.**

Water irises such as **Iris pseudacorus** *spp. are surface growers that require wide-mouthed pots to accommodate more than one year's growth. Usually growing two to three feet tall, they provide dramatic vertical form and romantic blooms in late spring and early summer.* **Photo by Greg Speichert.**

Iris versicolor and Iris virginica, *along with cross-species hybrids, follow the traditional surface growth pattern of water irises. Extra wide, shallow pots and regular feedings ensure healthy growth for more than one season in the same pot.* Photo by Greg Speichert.

Umbrella palms, Cyperus alternifolius spp., *form large clumps if given a suitably wide pot. Like many other aquatics, they do not require so much depth of soil as they do room to spread. Feed regularly for healthy growth.* Photo courtesy of Maryland Aquatic Nurseries.

Thalia *spp. offers canna-like blooms in a slower-growing plant. Hardy to a Zone 6, the plant offers tropical-looking foliage and charming summer blooms. It requires a bit more depth in the pot than other surface-growing plants, while still providing room for its clumping habit.* Photo by Greg Speichert.

Azolla *spp., a dainty floating plant, is not a favored food of fish. It will have to be controlled by netting out excess plants. With a nitrogen-fixing property, the excess plants make excellent additions to the compost pile.* Photo by Ronald E. Everhart.

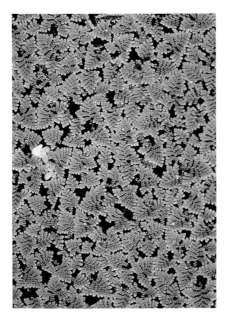

(Dichromena colorata) *White-topped sedge offers sparkling white starry tips that brighten the summer pond. Hardy only to Zones 8–11, it should be grown in a wide pot during the season and moved indoors to a sunny window for the colder winter months.* Photo by Greg Speichert.

LOW-MAINTENANCE PLANT & FISH CARE

Sagittaria *spp., such as this narrow-leaf form, can usually remain in the same roomy pot for two or three seasons. If the pot has holes in the bottom, the plant often escapes and sprouts from outside the pot.* Photo by Ronald E. Everhart.

MANAGING WATER HYACINTHS

To help control the prolific water hyacinth in the pond, fill a pot half-full of soil and lay in the plant's trailing roots. Photo by Oliver Jackson.

Fill the pot nearly full of soil while covering the hyacinth's roots. Tamp the soil to help anchor the plant and top with pea gravel. Photo by Oliver Jackson.

A floating ring keeps water hyacinth confined to one area. Photo by Robert Johnson.

Set the pot in the pond so that the plant floats on the water's surface. As new plantlets attain size, they can be snapped free and potted in the same manner. Photo by Oliver Jackson.

LOW-MAINTENANCE WATER LILIES

Water lilies delight the water garden. Many of the hardy water lilies commonly available, however, are of *odorata* rootstock or scrambling and vigorous habit. These lilies require not only large, heavy pots of soil, but can also require repotting each season. Larger-leaved lilies are not happy confined to small pots.

Some of the medium-size growers can be adapted to smaller container growth. Dwarf-type, pygmy species or tropical water lilies work best with smaller pots and may be kept within the same pot for more than one season.

Tradition has mandated that water lilies be planted in baskets

The delicate peach hue of N. 'Solfatare' is no small delight. **Photo by Ronald E. Everhart.**

or pots with holes, but commercial growers and hobbyists confirm that the lilies can be grown healthily in holeless pots. The lilies do require regular feeding, however.

N. *'Solfatare'* is a dwarf-type lily suited to the small water garden. Photo by Ronald E. Everhart.

Known as a "sunset" or changeable lily, N. 'Comanche' will display a distinct color change over its four-day life span. **Photo by Ronald E. Everhart.**

LOW-MAINTENANCE PLANT & FISH CARE

The slightest hint of blue in the red petals of N. 'James Brydon' captivates the lily enthusiast. Photo by Ronald E. Everhart.

The vibrant red of N. 'Escarboucle' makes for uncommon and surprising zest in the pond. Photo by Ronald E. Everhart.

N. *'Mme. Wilfon Gonnere' offers fully double, glowing pink blooms.* **Photo by Ronald E. Everhart.**

N. *'Comanche' is accompanied by lightly mottled leaves for even more interest in the pond.* **Photo by Ronald E. Everhart.**

A pristine white foil in the garden is offered by N. marliacea *'Albida.'* **Photo by Ronald E. Everhart.**

The diminutive N. 'Graziella' is not much bigger than the nearby Floating Heart. **Photo by Henry and Carol Reimer.**

LOW-MAINTENANCE WATER GARDENS

N. *'Chromatella' presents a cheery yellow presence that is happily confined to a smaller pot.* **Photo by Ronald E. Everhart.**

The white sepals of N. *'Attraction' frame its vivid hue.* **Photo by Ronald E. Everhart.**

N. *'Ellisiana' is a delightful dwarf-type red lily.* **Photo by Ronald E. Everhart.**

The pygmy lily 'Helvola' provides ready blooms among very small, mottled leaves. **Photo by Ronald E. Everhart.**

No bigger than a silver dollar, N. pygmaea 'Helvola' is suited to even the smallest of water gardens. Photo by Henry and Carol Reimer.

N. 'Indiana' is a delightful dwarf-type water lily. Photo by Ronald E. Everhart.

Another yellow lily for the smaller pot is the more lemony yellow N. 'Moorei.' Photo by Ronald E. Everhart.

Long a favorite among water gardeners, N. 'Attraction' adapts well to smaller pot plantings. Photo by Ronald E. Everhart.

Any tropical water lily, such as this pink seedling of N. 'Pamela,' grows well in a small container since the tropical rhizome does not scramble about the way many of its hardy cousins tend to grow. Photo by Ronald E. Everhart.

LOW-MAINTENANCE WATER GARDENS

This fourth-day bloom of N. *'Indiana' is markedly different from the changeable lily's first-day yellow bloom.* Photo by Ronald E. Everhart.

The tropical N. *'Dauben' offers a blue bloom in diminutive form.* Photo by Henry and Carol Reimer.

LOW-MAINTENANCE PLANT & FISH CARE

LOW-MAINTENANCE LOTUS

Lotuses are truly gorgeous aquatic plants. Most varieties commonly available, however, are standard-size and require very large pots. A school of thought is developing, however, that since the plants are surface rooters, they can be grown in much shallower soil. Providing the necessary growing room for the vigorous plant is not so unwieldy if the depth of soil can be significantly lessened. Likewise, growing the dwarf forms such as 'Momo Botan' or some of the new imported Chinese bowl lotuses may make the plant a viable possibility for the low-maintenance water garden.

Good news for the low-maintenance growing of lotus comes from both Longwood Gardens and Maryland Aquatic Nurseries. Lotuses probably need to be fed but once a season, instead of the several times monthly usually reported. An overfed lotus will display yellow leaves with green veining before finally dying.

N. *'Momo Botan' is a popular dwarf lotus that remains happy in a smaller pot.* **Photo courtesy of Maryland Aquatic Nurseries.**

Dwarf-type lotus, such as Hongbian bai wanlian, are more easily contained than their standard-sized counterparts. **Photo by Greg Speichert.**

SELECTING APPROPRIATE PLANTS

How often we fall in love with a plant pictured in a book! But is it a plant that will grow happily in our own pond? Primulas, for example, are given considerable attention in water garden books produced in Great Britain, where the climate is different from that of a similar latitude in the U.S. Comparable areas in the U.S. are too hot and dry for the successful growth of many primulas. Likewise, lotuses, requiring full sunlight and 90°F (32°C) temperatures for optimal growth do not perform as well in Great Britain. Submerged aquatics can be misleading, too. It would seem logical that a plant hardy in colder zones would do well in warmer zones. However, some plants are happier in cooler waters, just as some plants are happier in warmer waters. Trying to grow plants under less-than-ideal circumstances results in poor growth and more maintenance.

Before deciding upon plant varieties to include in the water garden, check with local nurserymen. If knowledgeable people are not available, check with several mail-order nurseries for their assessments.

ECO-BALANCE

Some confusion exists concerning the establishment of an eco-balance in the pond. Originally, such discussions were meant to illuminate the principles of creating a complete microcosm within a small man-made feature. In that sense, supplying the pond with as great a variety of life as possible enables a more complete eco-system to be developed and maintained. As the various systems are established, a natural balance is achieved. However, with the growing popularity of water gardening, establishing an eco-balance has come to be syn-

LOW-MAINTENANCE PLANT & FISH CARE

Submerged aquatics, such as
Elodea canadensis, *allow*
maintenance-free potting. Since
the plants gain most of their
nutrients from the water itself, it
is not necessary to pot them in soil.
Fill a pot half-full of pea gravel
and lay in the cut ends of the
plants. **Photo by Oliver Jackson.**

Fill around the plants with pea
gravel to anchor them within the
pot. **Photo by Oliver Jackson.**

Set the pot on the pond bottom.
The plants will form anchoring
roots as they help keep the water
free of green water algae. Snip
excess growth off with a fingernail
to propagate more plants. **Photo**
by Oliver Jackson.

onymous with creating a clear-water pond.

Formulas of x number of submerged aquatics, x number of marginal aquatics, x amount of surface coverage, and x number of scavengers make it seem these few factors create the desired eco-balance and clear water. An ecologically balanced pond may have clear water, but a pond with clear water may not be ecologically balanced. There are ways, such as the use of filtration or UV sterilizers, to clear water without having a "balanced" pond. In the final analysis, there is more than one way to set up a water garden.

Regardless of how much of everything else you put in your pond of the "formula," you will have naturally clear water if you put in one bunch (5–6 plants per bunch) of submerged aquatics per square foot of water surface, provided you haven't over-stocked the pond with fish. You may also discover that submerged plants aren't required at all if you have enough surface area for a good population of water hyacinths (*eichhornia crasipes*) and enough open area for oxygen exchanges. If both types of plants affect the pond's water clarity in the same way, remember that it is far easier to net out excess floating plants than to prune a plant growing on the bottom of the pond.

If your pond is large enough to establish a true eco-balance of plants, animals, insects, microbes, and water chemistry, pursue it. However, if it is too small, accept its limitations and do your best to satisfy your pond's requirements in whatever ways that are practical and feasible for you.

LOW MAINTENANCE AND FISH

The basic principle to follow for achieving low maintenance in fish care is to observe carefully the recommended stocking level for your pond. Putting too many fish in a pond will create considerable maintenance demands, water-quality problems, and the likelihood of diseased fish. Maximum fish stocking levels are given for water gardens in two forms: 3 to 5 inches (2–3.5 cm) of goldfish per gallon (liter) of water or 1 inch (28 cm) of goldfish per square foot (sq. m) of water surface. This maximum stocking rate is halved if you are keeping koi in the pond. Maintaining the fish load of your pond well below these maximum levels will help to ensure easy fish care.

FISH AND AMMONIA

Fish do grow and fish do spawn. Many baby fish escape the "food chain" and add to the resident population. Overnight you may find yourself faced with rising ammonia and nitrite levels from the fish overload. If you are observing the stocking level and keeping the pond clean of decomposing organic matter, it is not necessary to test the water frequently. However, water test kits are easy to use and should be kept on hand if your fish load is near capacity.

By keeping a white fish in the pond, you have a barometer of such conditions developing. A fish under stress first shows a rosy blushing in the fins and tail. With a white fish this is quickly apparent. As the stressful condition worsens, the fish develops red veining on its body. At this point, the fish is in serious jeopardy. If no parasites are readily apparent, immediately check the ammonia and nitrite levels in the pond and take corrective measures.

If your water supply adds ammonia to the water to create long-lived chloramines, you may need to deal with elevated ammonia levels even though the fish are stocked within acceptable levels. Call your water company

Zeolite in the form of chips aids in removing ammonia from the water. They may be used as a filter media in boxes attached to the submerged pump. **Photo by Oliver Jackson.**

Fancy goldfish, such as orandas with their air-filled caps, require more care and attention than common varieties of goldfish. **Photo courtesy of Blue Ridge Fish Hatchery.**

Butterfly koi are hardier and smaller fish than their Japanese koi relatives. **Photo courtesy of Blue Ridge Fish Hatchery.**

to ask if they use chloramines or add ammonia to the water, or test the water directly from the tap. Some public suppliers offer water from the tap with ammonia already at fish-toxic levels. If this is the case in your area, preventive action can avoid inevitable maintenance problems.

Keep zeolite or Ammo Chips™ on hand to deal with sudden, elevated ammonia levels. The mineral can serve as a filter media, too. When necessary, suspend nylon stockings containing the chips in the pond water. Ammo Rocks™ may also be used on the pond bottom. Using zeolite preventatively or at the first indication of ammonia presence lessens maintenance problems.

FISH AND NITRITE

Fish overloads can also result in elevated levels of nitrite. Nitrite affects fish more severely and quickly than elevated levels of ammonia, and the fish display the same signs of stress discussed above. Partial water changes with non-iodized dissolved salt at a ratio of 2.5 pounds (1 k) per 100 gallons (350 l) detoxify nitrite. Remove the fish to safer waters if the water tests deadly toxic. These actions consume time and energy. The low-maintenance pond avoids the situation by monitoring the fish load and using a simple bio-filter to ensure nitrification of fish wastes.

The small, colorful White Cloud fish is suited to life in the warmer tropical pond. **Photo courtesy of Nick Romanowski.**

FISH AND CHLORINE

Chlorine, harmful to both fish and plants, is a fact of life in most municipal water supplies. Spraying the water into the pond dissipates the volatile gas. However, water additions of only five percent of the pond's volume are not likely to affect either the fish or the plants. Commercial products that neutralize the chlorine are available from pet shops.

FISH AND PARASITES

A healthy fish usually withstands the attacks of both parasites and protozoan infestations. This is another reason to keep the fish stocking level low; fish stressed by crowded conditions lose their protective slime coating.

Parasitic and disease attacks commonly occur with seasonal changes in water temperatures. Especially after a winter's hibernation, fish are more susceptible to attack. Keeping your fish healthy and following preventative guidelines will help to prevent pond-size problems.

Anchor worm appears as tiny, white, sticklike protrusions attached to the fish. Remove them with tweezers, swab the wound with mercurochrome, dip the fish in a salt bath, and return it to the water or a hospital tank, observing the fish for any development of secondary fungal infection. An unpleasant chore, treating for anchor worms involves time and hassle.

Understanding the life-cycle of the parasite helps to prevent the problem. The parasite may be introduced into the pond by birds. If you enjoy birds around your yard, provide them their own nearby source of water to discourage them from taking a dip in the water garden.

Anchor worms may also be introduced on new fish or in the transport water of the new fish. New pond fish should be quarantined for a week to 10 days to be certain no parasites or diseases are introduced. Likewise, transport water should not be added to the pond since it can harbor the free-swimming stage of parasites. Once the water temperature has equalized between the transport water and the pond, move the fish by hand.

A hospital tank need be nothing more than an aquarium fitted with an aeration pump and an air stone. **Photo by Oliver Jackson.**

Equipping a hospital tank involves supplying zeolite to help control ammonia waste along with a stress-coat product to replace the fish's important slime coating. **Photo by Oliver Jackson.**

LOW-MAINTENANCE PLANT & FISH CARE

Often medical treatments for fish are temperature-dependent. Affixing a thermometer to the aquarium glass helps assure proper dosages and administration. **Photo by Oliver Jackson.**

Snails serve as an intermediary host for the parasite. It may be necessary to remove them from the pond if parasites are present.

The most common protozoan infestation of fish is ich, evidenced by tiny white spots on the fish's skin. Treatment for ich should be done in a hospital tank where high salt or chemical treatments will not impact the pond or be so costly.

If a fish shows signs of a problem, the easiest way to tend to it is to remove the fish from the pond to a hospital tank. This need be nothing more than a small aquarium outfitted with an aeration stone or filter. Do not include activated carbon in the filter since it quickly removes any medications.

NEW FISH FOR THE POND

Disease and parasites occur in the most reputable of fish hatcheries and pet shops. Any new fish to be introduced to the pond should be quarantined for seven to 10 days in a hospital tank before being placed in the pond. Because the life cycle of parasites and disease is temperature-dependent, such a period allows sufficient time for problems to present themselves. Should a problem become apparent, several treatments will be necessary over the parasite's life cycle, as determined by the tank's water temperature. Detecting and treating problems before the fish is put into the pond prevents whole-pond contamination, costly treatments, heartache, and hassle.

To successfully keep healthy koi, careful attention must be paid to water quality. **Photo by Lee Dreyfuss.**

SIGNS OF FISH PROBLEMS

A fish can't talk and a fish can't bark, but it can tell you when something is wrong. The following signs indicate something amiss:

• Loss of appetite

• Fins clamped close to body

• Swimming weakly close to the water's surface or off by itself

• Being nipped or bumped by other fish when they are not spawning

• Increased gill movements

• Changes in the appearance of fins, skin, or eyes

• Increased mucous production on body

• Blushing of fins or red streaking on body

• Scratching on pond walls, rocks, etc. (flashing)

• Jumping from the water or out of the pond when not spawning

Watch the fish closely if any of these signals are given. In general, if the fish continues to feed, the problem is likely to be parasitic. If the fish is no longer interested in feeding, the problem may be protozoan. For the low-maintenance pond, prevention is the key to these problems. Keep the number of fish on the low side and keep the pond clean. Detritus collecting on the pond bottom makes an excellent incubator for problems!

FISH AND OXYGEN

The primary source of oxygen in your pond is the pond's surface, where it contacts the air. Too much surface coverage creates lowered oxygen levels, particularly at night when oxygen levels fall due to plant uptake. Especially during the heat of summer when the water warms significantly and is unable to hold as much oxygen, fishes gasping at the surface are not being "friendly" and they are probably not hungry. They want oxygen.

If you have a recycling pump running in the pond, leave it running all night. If the fish still seem to require more oxygen, set up an aeration stone or a mister

Feeding fish a food that has little particle dust prevents contamination and clouding of the water from excess organic decomposition. **Photo by Oliver Jackson.**

LOW-MAINTENANCE PLANT & FISH CARE

An easy way to keep track of floating food fed to your fish: a floating form that confines the food to one area. Any food remaining after the feeding period is readily netted from the pond. **Photo by H. Nash.**

that will also help cool too-warm water. Thinning out surface-covering plants may also be advised. These are simple preventative actions that can help avoid frantic efforts to determine why your fish are suddenly floating lifelessly in the pond.

FEEDING YOUR FISH

If your pond is established and large enough, enough insect larvae and micro-organisms probably exist to satisfy the appetites of your fish. Very small pre-

formed ponds may not offer such a smorgasborg. Koi, also, tend to need more food than goldfish. However, problems with water quality (excess ammonia and nitrite) develop if you overfeed your fish, the excess food becoming organic pond waste. Most experts recommend feeding only what your fish will eat in five to 10 minutes and then netting out any excess. Obviously, such feeding involves floating fish foods. For your fishes' health, soak the food briefly before feeding it, to prevent digestive problems created by the food's expansion within the digestive tract. A truly low-maintenance way of feeding fish is to use the floating ring, seen so often in koi-keepers' ponds. If the fish food is confined to the floating ring, it cannot become lost among plants or around the pond edges.

FISH SELECTION

Some breeds of fish require more care than others. Deep-bodied goldfish, especially those with bubble features, such as orandas, are more sensitive to water quality and require more attention to their feeding and health. Orfe, too, while requiring a large pond and being kept low in number, are more sensitive to water quality than other breeds. Koi, of course, require more room and more dietary attention than goldfish. The common goldfish, shubunkin, and comet goldfish are the most forgiving of pond fish. However, they are cold-water fish and may become stressed with lengthy periods in hot waters. Tropical or semi-tropical fish may be a more appropriate selection.

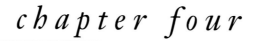

chapter four

LOW–
MAINTENANCE
TIPS

Creating a small stream within a gravel base minimizes maintenance. **Photo by T.J. Smith.**

Although prevention is the key to low-maintenance water gardening, there are many shortcuts to make the work more enjoyable and less time-consuming. Many of these techniques are the products of innovative companies, while others are the creative innovations of backyard hobbyists.

SEASONAL MAINTENANCE: SPRING

For the tropical water garden, spring means little more than a continuation of the day before. However, plants that rested show renewed vigor and need to have their feedings resumed. Likewise, plants that have filled out their pots require repotting and division.

The temperate-zone water garden awakens in the spring and requires more tending. If the pond was cleaned properly the preceeding autumn, a total draining and cleaning is not necessary. Cut off any dead foliage as the new growth resumes. Divide and repot plants that fill out their pots. Begin feeding those that can remain in their pots for another season.

If the water turns green before submerged plants can effectively compete with the algae for the nutrients or before the bio-filter can be restarted, practice patience. Move any submerged plants closer to the water's surface where they will gain more sunlight and grow more quickly. Water lilies may also gain a head start in this way. Avoid using water dyes that darken the water—the same shading action that inhibits algae growth will also inhibit desirable plant growth. Water lilies that have not sent growth to the surface may die for lack of sunlight. The tiny duckweed plant (*Lemna* sp.) flourishes in the early spring and proves helpful in spring algae-bloom control.

Sometimes it is not necessary to divide a lily. The lily may be moved with its soil-ball intact to a larger pot, with fresh soil filling out the new container. **Photo by T.J. Smith.**

LOW-MAINTENANCE WATER GARDENS

A wheelbarrow is a handy means of keeping the potting supplies together. **Photo by T.J. Smith.**

A fine-mesh swimming pool skimmer will remove floating algae. **Photo by Oliver Jackson.**

Plants that were grown in small pots can be transplanted into larger pots with their soil-ball intact. This will save time until the next year, when a proper division and repotting can be performed.

Once the water has stabilized to around 55°F (13°C), resume feeding the fish. Start with an easily digested wheat-germ food. Watch for parasitic or protozoan infestations. Take action as necessary.

Instead of draining the pond, perform a partial water change using a pond vacuum to clean any mulm or sediment that accumulated over the winter. Treat for chlorine if necessary.

Check the water quality as the season begins. If ammonia or nitrite problems are present, take appropriate steps to alleviate them.

Remove any pumps used through the winter and hose them clean. When the water temperature reaches 55°F (13°C), start up the bio-filter.

SEASONAL MAINTENANCE: SUMMER

Low-maintenance summer water gardening means using either a good filter or enough submerged or floating plants to keep the pond nutrients under control. Check particle filters occasionally for clogs that require hosing.

Monitor fish spawning from spring on, to be certain their numbers do not exceed the pond's capacity. Give fish floating foods high in protein. Feed only what they will eat in 5–10 minutes and net out any excess.

Divide plants that are filling out their pots and repot in wide-mouthed pots. Remove dying

A selection of tools that might assist with pond maintenance includes large and small nets, a fine-mesh skimmer, pruning shears, and a hoe. **Photo by Karla Anderson.**

foliage to minimize the pond's bio-load.

Make water changes if desired, but do not change more than five percent of the total pond volume and keep it to no more than once weekly, to avoid dechlorination. Water changes made with a pond vacuum remove settled organic solids that might create a haven for parasite eggs or anaerobic bacteria.

Watch for aphid attacks, and hose them into the water for the fish to eat. If this method does not work, mix a bit of dishwashing detergent in a spray bottle of vegetable oil. The soap emulsifies the oil, which then suffocates the insects. If the oil covers

Other useful tools for pond maintenance are a basket with screening for the submerged pump, hose splitters, a cushion to kneel upon, a plastic broom, and a putty knife. **Photo by Cliff Tallman.**

the water surface, remove it once it has done its job. Leaving the oil film on the water prevents oxygen exchanges. Remove the oil film by flooding the pond or by soaking it up with paper towels.

Moths or beetles may attack water lilies. Control light infestations by removing affected leaves. For severe infestations, remove the plants to a separate tub to treat with appropriate insecticides. Never spray insecticides, herbicides, or copper sulfate into the pond itself. Potassium permanganate, to a plum color, can also be used in the treatment tub for parasitic control. Various forms of Bt (*Bacillus thuringiensis*) are available to use with caterpiller or grub-type larvae. The bacteria must come into contact with the pest in order to parasitize and kill it. Bt is safe for use in the pond itself.

If the fish gasp at the surface, provide more oxygen. Leave the pump running all night or add aeration with an air pump and air stone. Be certain that surface coverage is not excessive—a general rule of thumb being no more than 60 percent of the pond's surface.

Keep an eye on the pond during very hot spells. A tent over part of the pond helps prevent overheated water. Additional aeration may be advisable, as might spraying or misting the water's

Ground cover plants can make for easy maintenance. **Photo by H. Nash.**

LOW-MAINTENANCE TIPS

Combining stone, mulch, flagstone, and deck walkways with ground cover plants creates an attractive low-maintenance setting. **Photo by Oliver Jackson.**

A simple hatch door makes it easy to access the pond below. **Photo by Jim Martinson.**

LOW-MAINTENANCE WATER GARDENS

surface to assist with cooling and aeration. The supplemental aeration and gentle cooling efforts are warranted if most of the pond surface is covered with plants, thereby trapping heat within the pond. Do not add great amounts of cold water, because the sudden temperature change can stress or kill fish.

LOW MAINTENANCE: AUTUMN

Tropical pond owners may notice even tropical plants slowing their growth during the autumn months. Stop feeding the plants to allow this respite. Hardy plants should be trimmed back as they die to deny overwintering quarters for insect pests, as well as to prevent adding to the pond's bio-load.

Pond owners in freezing zones should move hardy plants that should not freeze, such as water lilies, parrot's feather, and some varieties of arrowhead and pickerel weed, below the anticipated ice level. Tropical plants should be removed from the pond before the first frost. Bring tropical marginal plants into the house as houseplants; place potted tropical lilies in plastic bags that will prevent their drying out, or put them in shallow tubs of water in a cool, dark, non-freezing location.

Prevent leaves from falling into the pond and settling to the bottom. Providing a screen, net, or shadecloth cover during leaf-fall prevents backaches and water-quality problems.

As the weather cools, feed fish wheat-germ foods, which are more easily digested by slowing digestive systems. Soak the food before feeding. Taper the feedings to once every few days until the temperature stabilizes at 50°F (10°C), when feeding stops altogether.

At the same time, clean out and store the bio-filter for the winter. Bio-filters in climates where the winter temperatures will not go below 50°F (10°C) can be maintained throughout the year. Clean the submersible pump and either store it or set it up close to the pond's surface, where its bubbling action at the surface prevents complete freezing. By moving the pump up

Fully lining a stream and waterfall course prevents water loss and extensive maintenance. **Photo by Oliver Jackson.**

Mulch around the pond reduces ground maintenance. **Photo by Greg Jones.**

Water recycled through a pipe affords the sound of moving water in a simple design. **Photo by H. Nash, courtesy of Firehouse Image Center, Indianapolis.**

from the lower depths, the fish will not be disturbed by water temperature changes.

Use the pond vacuum one last time to remove organic matter that might produce fish-toxic gases during the winter. If this has been removed and the pond surface should happen to freeze over for short periods, the fish should be safe. This last vacuuming will also help prevent the spring algae bloom that might feed on nutrients produced by the decomposing organic matter.

LOW MAINTENANCE: WINTER

Tropical ponds will take a breather while the plants rest briefly. Bottom vacuuming may be performed as needed. If the weather cools into the fifties (10–15°C), cut back on the amount of food fed to fish. Keep dying vegetation trimmed off. Perennial plants may need to be cut fully back to encourage new growth in the spring. Protect the tropical plants during cold spells by rigging a plastic tent over at least part of the pond.

Ponds that freeze on occasion should have provisions for a hole to be kept open in the ice. Keep the pump running at the water's surface; float rubber balls or Styrofoam; or use a pond de-icer or livestock water heater. Fish will not suffer during brief freezing periods if the pond has been well cleaned.

Decreased spring maintenance results when the pond is protected during the winter by a plastic tent. **Photo by Ron Everhart.**

Allowing the submerged pump to bubble at the water's surface keeps a hole open in the ice in all but the coldest of weather. This allows any toxic gases to escape and protects the health of fish. **Photo by Ronald E. Everhart.**

VACUUMING
THE POND

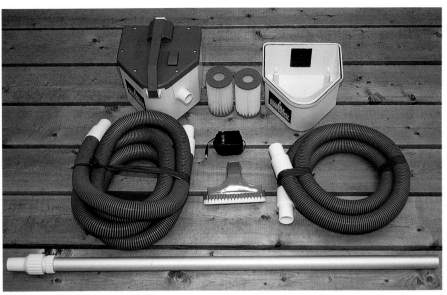

Pond vacuums may come in several parts that make for easier storage between uses. **Photo by Oliver Jackson.**

Accu Clear™ promotes the clotting of fine particle matter, facilitating its removal from the water. **Photo courtesy of Aquarium Pharmaceuticals.**

The new Odyssey™ vacuum operates by rechargeable battery, making it easy to use with no electrical outlet nearby. The unit floats in the water. **Photo by Oliver Jackson.**

LOW-MAINTENANCE TIPS

The discharge hose of the vacuum is directed from the pond into an area that will accept temporary flooding. **Photo by Oliver Jackson.**

Bottom sediment quickly disappears with a slow movement of the vacuum hose. **Photo by Oliver Jackson.**

GENERAL MAINTENANCE TIPS

TOOLS AND EQUIPMENT

Much of the hassle of pond maintenance can be lessened simply by having appropriate tools and equipment on hand. Here is a brief list:

• Water test kit (ammonia, nitrite, and pH) (chlorine test, if necessary)

• Fish net, for netting out fish

• Fine-meshed leaf skimmer, for removing floating debris or particulate matter from the pond bottom

• Pond vacuum, siphon or battery-operated, for removing sediment from pond bottom

• Five-gallon bucket, for holding fish or plants or dissolving bacteria

• Scrub brush, for cleaning pump and pond as needed

• Bottle brush, for twirling out filamentous algae

• Five–10 gallon aquarium, filter optional, to be used as a hospital or quarantine tank

• Air pump and air stone, for supplying supplemental aeration to pond or hospital tank

• Commercial dechlorinator or sodium thiosulfate, if water is chlorinated

• One pound of non-iodized salt, for fish treatments in the hospital tank

• Ammo Chips™ or zeolite, for emergency treatment of ammonia in pond, filter, or hospital tank

• Mercurochrome, for treating fish wounds

• Bt (*Bacillus thuringiensis*), for killing destructive insect larvae

• Spray bottle, for mixing soap and oil in aphid treatment

• Plant fertilizer, either aquatic plant tablets or liquid

• Floating pellet or stick fish food

• Long-handled snipping or pruning shears, for trimming dying leaves in the pond from the outside

• Pond repair kit, for repairing punctures

• Dry-form nitrifying bacteria, for adding to filter or pond to jump-start, increase, or to replace bacteria as needed

• Strong, adjustable hose nozzle, for cleaning plants and spraying water into the pond

• Plastic bags, for collecting debris from the pond

Plastic milk crates make suitable plant pedestals without taking up valuable water space for fish. Using hanging basket planters may make the plants more accessible. **Photo by Oliver Jackson.**

PLANT PEDESTALS

Some aquatic plants need to be elevated within the pond. Concrete blocks or cinder blocks can raise the pond's pH and are quite heavy. Stacking bricks can also be a heavy and back-stressing chore. While plastic milk or storage crates float in the water, the weight of a potted plant holds them down.

ESTABLISHING SUBMERGED AQUATICS

Most fish nibble on tender-leaved submerged aquatics. And while koi are notorious for foraging in plant toppings in search of larval delicacies, goldfish, too, engage in this behavior. Freshly planted submerged aquatics are easily uprooted. To help estab-lish the plants, enclose the entire pot and plant within plastic mesh. Mesh onion bags are readily available in the supermarket. In the presence of large fish, submerged aquatics remain safe grown inside the plastic crates used as plant pedestals. (If such plantings must be long-term, select shade-tolerant plants such as *cabomba*.)

Using mulch and stone, and perhaps a rock garden in the process, affords easy maintenance. **Photo by T.J. Smith.**

PLANT MAINTENANCE

Entering the pond to remove dying vegetation may be done monthly without too much decomposing vegetation accumulating. Long-handled pruning shears may be used, also. Remove the clippings with a leaf skimmer.

REMOVING BOTTOM DEBRIS

Pond vacuums, used in conjunction with partial water changes of up to 25 percent of the pond volume, keep the pond healthy and clean. A fine-meshed leaf skimmer can also scoop debris from the bottom.

WINTERING TROPICAL WATER LILIES

If the lilies are potted in holeless pots, they can be wintered in the same pot by simply keeping the pot topped off with water or by submerging it in shallow water during the winter months. The potted lily may also be stored in a plastic bag that prevents it from drying out. Store the lily in a cool, non-freezing place such as a garage, basement, or inside closet. Stick a note on the refrigerator door to remind yourself to check the water level. A dry lily is a dead lily.

WARM SPELLS IN WINTER

People in cold regions delight in the occasional warm spell that arrives like a gift in the midst of winter. Fish, too, sense the excitement and move around more than usual, perhaps even wandering about the pond's surface. Don't give in to the temptation to feed them—their metabolisms are too slow to properly digest food, although they might think it's a good idea at the time. Wait until the temperatures have warmed to a consistent 50°F + (10°C +) before feeding them again.

Mulch combined with repetition of the pond's flagstone edging into the surrounding area is easy to tend. **Photo by T.J. Smith.**

FROGS AND TURTLES IN THE POND

Part of the delight of a water garden is the variety of aquatic life that can live there. Fish are not the only life that can live in the pond. Toads will breed in the backyard pond but will not remain tadpoles very long. Before the season is over, they leave the pond and scout for food in the garden. Frogs may move into the pond. Especially if hatched and grown there or accompanied by a mate, they may remain. Small tadpoles will be eaten by larger fish, just as small fish will be eaten by frogs. If you wish baby fish to survive in the same pond inhabited by frogs, net out the babies and keep them indoors in an aquarium until they are large enough to have a chance of survival. Supplementing the frog's diet with earthworms may help, but it will not convince the frog that fish are not tasty.

Dwarf plants tucked into crevices and gaps in stonework discourage weeds. **Photo by T.J. Smith.**

Turtles can be a delightful addition to the pond. As babies, they present no significant increase in pond maintenance. They should have a flat area provided for their necessary sunning and should be fed appropriately. Once they become adults, however, problems arise. Adult turtles eat fish as well as plants. Their waste products become more of a consideration, too, especially in the small water garden. Adult turtles may need more appropriate homes to spend their long lives in than low-maintenance water gardens.

Frogs are part of the fun and surprise in a pond, but remember they do eat fish. **Photo by Ronald E. Everhart.**

TENDING SMALL FISH IN THE POND

Michigan water gardener Cliff Tallman places new small fish in a floating basket with small holes in it. The small fish gain the benefit of living in the pond with the assurance of being fed enough while being kept safe from larger fish. Cliff has noted that when the babies are large enough to fend for themselves, they simply jump out of the basket.

Establishing grass between flagstones makes for less maintenance than a full lawn surround. **Photo by H. Nash.**

A sandy beach offers both design and low maintenance. **Photo by Cliff Tallman.**

FEEDING FISH FRY

Baby fish are known as fry. The first couple days after hatching, the translucent fry feed by absorbing their yolk sacs. For the next week, they can be fed commercial baby foods or hard-boiled egg yolks. Following that week, you can crush flaked fish food into very fine particles. The flake foods should have at least 42 percent protein content. Of course, if you have kept a container of water off in the shade somewhere, especially one with a few crushed leaves in it, you may find that you have enough *daphnia*, or water fleas, to feed to the new little ones.

ALGAE-EATING PLECOSTOMUS

Aquarium owners are familiar with the algae-eating Plecostomus. He can be very useful in the summer or tropical pond. If you do not want to winter him indoors, the local pet store may be willing to take him

Stepping-stones to set amid gravel are available in creative designs to express humor, whimsy, or personality.
Photo by Karla Anderson.

and trade him in for a new one the following spring.

A HEAD-START BIO-FILTER IDEA

Areas of short summers can get a head start with a bio-filter by beginning it indoors. Set up a plastic container with a small recycling pump in the bottom. Cover the pump with your bio-filter media. Fill the container to cover the media. Season the water with some pond water, too. Rig the return to the side of the container. Dissolve the dry bacteria and add them to the recycling water in the media tub. Keep the pump running around the clock. After a couple weeks, the bacteria will be well established for moving into the outdoor bio-filter.

COMBINING CHORES

Irrigation of a nearby flower bed or lawn can be combined with topping off the pond. Compensate for normal pond evaporation by combining the two chores with a sprinkler head.

BEWARE OF COPPER FIXTURES

A sure sign that copper is leaching into the pond water from copper fountains and fixtures is an aqua-blue cast to the water. At the same time, you're likely to notice plants yellowing quickly with the lower plants, such as submerged aquatics, dying. Fish are affected, too, losing their slime-coat protection and falling prey to infestations or disease.

DEALING WITH pH READINGS

While pH levels in the pond are not normally a problem, it is a good idea to know the normal reading for your water supply. Perform this testing on the pond's water source. Compare that reading to the pond reading. The pond reading may be slightly different from its source's because of an algae bloom or the presence of lime in mortar or concrete. Algae blooms can produce fluctuations in the reading if the water pH is below 7. Buffer the water to alleviate swings in pH levels by placing natural limestone in the pond water.

Pond pH readings at 8.5 or above indicate the presence of lime in the water from mortar or concrete in and around the pond. All such pieces of lime should be removed and the exposed lime neutralized.

The sound of moving water is achieved with a simple carved rock and basin. **Photo by H. Nash.**

Lawn edging attractively separates lawn and pond. **Photo courtesy of Kinsman Company.**

pH readings at 10 or higher are toxic to fish, but readings above neutral will amplify the toxicity of any ammonia or nitrite tenfold for each integer on the pH scale. If the pH reading is normally high but still under the lime-indicative 8.5, monitor the pond regularly for ammonia and nitrite toxicity to avoid fish-toxic conditions.

After concrete or mortar removal, lower the pH reading by no more than 0.2 during any 24-hour period in the presence of fish. This will prevent life-threatening conditions for them. The pH can be lowered by sprinkling clear vinegar into the water and monitoring the effect of each addition.

If you lower the pH chemically, be certain the chemical is not a phosphate-based acid that will add more phosphates to the pond—perhaps resulting in green water.

FLOATING ALGAE

Scummy patches of floating algae can be removed with a long-handled fine-meshed skimmer. Looking closely into the water, you may notice, too, that cloudy patches of algae are developing. Filter through a fine-mesh medium, add enough submerged plants to deprive the growing algae of nutrients, or set up a UV sterilizer.

KEEPING LEAVES FROM THE POND

PVC frames that are easily dismantled for storage can be made to fit the pond. Landscaping shadecloth fitted onto the frames provides protection from leaves falling into the pond. Double wooden forms with fabric screening stapled in between can be made for smaller ponds. Long

Kits to create walkways make do-it-yourself projects around the pond easy to accomplish. **Photo courtesy of Walkmaster Company.**

LOW-MAINTENANCE TIPS

A brick paver path set within
mulch creates a carefree pond
surrounding. **Photo by**
T.J. Smith.

2×4's can also be placed across the pond with netting rolled across them. Bridal veil tulle is an inexpensive netting and is fine enough to catch pine needles.

BEATING THE SUMMER HEAT

If the return hose on the recycling pump is equivalent to a garden hose or an adapter can be fitted to the end of the tubing, attach a misting device to the hose return to recycle water as a cooling mist.

A sheet of Styrofoam floated on the pond during hot sunny days provides welcome shade relief to the finned inhabitants below.

MORE STYROFOAM USES

Float a piece of Styrofoam to provide welcome shade during the early spring before aquatic plants are growing. Likewise, in winter, a Styrofoam sheet keeps the pond from freezing solid in cold climates.

DON'T FORGET THAT THE WATER'S RUNNING

Monumental disasters can occur if you forget about the water running into the pond, especially if the water is chlorinated. Jan Noel-Smith, a Southern koi keeper, recommends turning on the oven timer to go off in a period of time to remind yourself to check the water. She sets it again for another 15 minutes later to verify the fishes are not stressing from the change. (Water companies do add strange chemicals sometimes!) Jan also sets her timer if she is draining the pond, to avoid burning out the pump from a lack of water.

To safely rake gravel covering pond liners, use the back side of the rake. **Photo by Oliver Jackson.**

Fish feeder blocks, similar to ones used in aquariums, allow worry-free vacations. **Photo courtesy of Aquarium Pharmaceuticals.**

POND BABYSITTERS

If you need to be away from home for several days, you might ask a neighbor to monitor the water level of your pond. Leave instructions that water be added only if the water drops to a certain point. (Your neighbor might not have an oven timer.) Unless the neighbor is accustomed to feeding pond fish, it may be best to let the fish feed on available food within the pond or from a floating, vacation feeder available from the pet store.

VACUUMING A DIRTY POND BOTTOM

Regular maintenance using a skimmer to clean the debris from the pond bottom will usually keep the pond fairly clean through the season. However, in the autumn or spring, you may find yourself wanting to fully vacuum and clean the pond bottom. If much sediment and debris have collected, move the fish to temporary quarters until the job is completed. Thick layers of debris may contain toxic gases from anaerobic bacteria working in them that can harm the fish. Watch for very small fish hiding among the debris.

SALT FOR ALGAE CONTROL

Many koi-keepers add 25 pounds (55 k) of non-iodized salt per 1000 gallons (3800 l) of water to kill spring algae blooms. This level of salt in the water acts as a

In spite of bad publicity, cats do not frequently bother the pond's fish. Creating a significant edge overhang or using loose gravel among the set stones will discourage inquisitive felines. **Photo by T.J. Smith.**

tonic to the fish and will not harm them. It will also kill most parasites. However, some aquatic plants are severely distressed by the salt and appear to die. Many will come back, but to keep them safe, move the stressed ones to temporary holding tubs. Once the salt has performed its job, begin partial water changes to clear its strength from the water. Salt does not dissipate in water; it must be flushed out of the system. Remember, too, to vacuum out the sedimentary settling of the dead algae.

LOW-MAINTENANCE LANDSCAPING IDEAS

Nothing is more time-consuming than pulling weeds from between rocks around the

A combination of pond treatments offers low maintenance — mulch, grass, flagstone, and decorative stone. **Photo courtesy of Maryland Aquatic Nurseries.**

pond or having to skim grass cuttings from the pond's surface before they start adding to the pond's nutrient-load.

During pond construction, the liner can be left extended further out from the pond than the usual few inches so it can act as a weed barrier. If the pond is already constructed, the immediate area can be dug out enough to lay a weed barrier.

Biobarrier®, manufactured by Reemay, Inc., in Old Hickory, Tennessee, offers a long-term weed-control solution. Nodules containing trifluralin are fixed into a porous landscape fabric. Strong enough to last through several seasons, the fabric allows moisture, air, and nutrients to pass through while creating a two-inch (5 cm) zone where surface vegetation will not grow. Shrubs and tree roots below the zone are unaffected. The product is especially effective with just a covering of mulch or decorative stone over it. Since most ponds have slightly raised edges and the chemical has a toxicity rating less than table salt and a water solubility of an extremely low 0.3 ppm, it is unlikely to leach into the pond water.

Instead of replacing the soil, use mulch or decorative stone. Bricks can be set in a thick sand base to make a paved surround, as can flagstone or other flat pavers. Many garden centers now offer concrete squares that are made to look like smaller bricks and stone pieced together. These larger sections offer less opportunity for weed growth. And, of course, concrete can be poured as a patio-type surround. The ideal objective is to surround the pond with an area that is easy to patrol for weeds.

COMMON SENSE

Low maintenance entails more than finding less-time-consuming ways of keeping the water garden; it also encompasses ways of easing the physical chores. Often common sense is the key. Provide back support in lifting heavy pots by using your legs instead of your back—squat when lifting heavy objects. Back problems may mean work inside the pond is limited to warm enough days for sitting or squatting in the water. Likewise, using long-poled skimmers from the pond edge may be better tolerated by sitting in a chair during the chore.

If you must go into the pond, wear rubber-soled canvas shoes to help prevent slipping. Wear

them, too, if rocks or pavings around the pond might be wet. Move potted plants that may complicate your entry and exit. Set plants on the pond edge rather than holding them as you climb out. Keep a plastic bag

handy, perhaps fixed to a belt, to collect debris.

Remember, too, the devices that are used in other gardening chores: back braces, gardening benches and seats, knee pillows, rubber gloves, and work tables.

PREDATOR PROTECTION

Predator netting serves as a low- maintenance fence. **Photo by Mary Kerns.**

Tub gardens may be raccoon-proofed with chicken-wire covers. **Photo by Ronald E. Everhart.**

In cases of persistent raccoons, put heavier grades of mechanics' wire over the pond. **Photo by H. Nash.**

The great blue heron apparently recognizes the alligator as an enemy and will avoid a pond adorned with a plastic reptile. Photo by T.J. Smith.

LOW-MAINTENANCE TIPS

HELPFUL INFORMATION

COMPUTING POOL VOLUME IN GALLONS

1. Mathematical formulas
   a. If computed in inches, divide the total by 231.
   b. If computed in feet, multiply the total by 7.5.
   Rectangular shapes: length × width × depth.
   Circular shapes: 3.14 × radius^2 × depth.
2. Using a domestic water meter: Use a wrench to turn the locking nut on the meter to remove the lid. Record the reading before filling the pool. Subtract this figure from the figure recorded after filling is completed. No water at all should be used in the house during filling.
3. Using hose output: Fill a large bucket for exactly 60 seconds. Measure the water in pints and divide by 8 to compute U.S. gallons. Record start and stop times of filling the pool. Multiply the total minutes required for filling by the number of gallons the hose discharges in one minute.

COMPUTING POOL VOLUME IN LITERS

1. Multiply length × width × depth in meters × 28.41 for rectangular volume.
2. Multiply depth in meters × metric diameter^2 × 20.75 for circular volume.

COMPUTING SURFACE AREA OF POOL

1. Rectangular shape: Multiply length × width.
2. Circular shape: Multiply half the diameter by itself for the radius squared. Multiply that by 3.14.

FREQUENTLY USED EQUIVALENTS

ppm (parts per million) is equivalent to one milligram per liter of water
5 ml = 1 tsp.*
20 drops = 1 ml
60 drops = 1 tsp.
15 ml = 1 tbsp.*
2 tsp. = 1 dessert spoon
2 dessert spoons = 1 tbsp.
2 tbsp. = 1 fl. oz.
8 fl. oz. = 1 cup
1 cup = 48 tsp.
1 cup = 16 tbsp.
1 cup = 237 ml
*These figures are commonly supplied by most chart sources. However, using a standard, pharmacist-supplied, two-milliliter eye dropper and a standard kitchen measuring teaspoon, the equivalency was found to be 3 ml/tsp. and 9 ml/tbsp.

MATHEMATICS OF CONVERSIONS

To Convert	Multiply by	To Obtain
inches	2.54	centimeters
inches	25.4	millimeters
feet	30	centimeters
millimeters	0.04	inches
grams	0.035	ounces
ounces	28	grams
pounds	0.45	kilograms
milliliters	0.03	fluid ounces
liters	2.1	pints
liters	1.06	quarts
liters	0.26	U.S. gallons
fluid ounces	30	milliliters
U.S. gallons	3.8	liters

Celsius to Fahrenheit: Multiply by 9, divide by 5, add 32.

Fahrenheit to Celsius: Subtract 32, multiply by 5, divide by 9.

TABLE OF LIQUID EQUIVALENTS

1 milliliter (ml) = 1 cm³
 = 1 cc
 = 20 drops
 = 0.20 tsp.
 = 0.061 in.³
 = 0.001 l
 = 1 gm of water
 = 0.002 lb. of water
 = 0.0003 U.S. gal.

1 fluid ounce (oz.) = 6 tsp.
 = 2 tbsp.
 = 0.0078 U.S. gal.

 = 0.031 qt.
 = 29.57 gm
 = 0.062 pt.
 = 0.065 lb.
 = 1.04 oz.
 = 1.8 in.³
 = 29.57 cc
 = 29.57 ml
 = 0.0296 l

1 liter (l) = 1000 ml
 = 1000 cm³
 = 1.7598 liquid pts.
 = 1.057 liquid qts.
 = 0.264 U.S. gal.
 = 203 tsp.
 = 67.6 tbsp.
 = 35.28 oz.
 = 33.8 fl. oz.
 = 4.23 cups
 = 2.1134 pt.
 = 2.205 lb.
 = 61.025 in.³
 = 0.0353 ft.³
 = 1000 gm
 = 1 kg of water

1 U.S. gallon (gal.) = 3.785 l
 = 0.1339 ft.³
 = 231 in.³
 = 8.345 lb. of water
 = 3785.4 gm of water
 = 4 qt.
 = 8 pt.
 = 135.52 oz.
 = 128 fl. oz.
 = 3785.4 ml

APPENDIX

Imperial gallon = 4.5459 l
  = 0.1605 ft.³
  = 277.42 in.³
  = 4.845 qt.

1 kiloliter (kl) = 1000 l
  = 264.18 gal.
  = 35.315 ft.³

  = 0.12 gal.
  = 0.016 ft.³ of water
  = 0.48 qt.
  = 0.96 pt.
  = 15.35 fl. oz.
  = 458.59 cc or cm³
  = 453.59 ml
  = 453.59 gm
  = 0.454 l

WEIGHT EQUIVALENTS

1 grain (gr.) = 64.8 mg
  = 0.065 gm
  = 0.35 oz.

1 gram (gm) = 15.432 gr.
  = 0.0353 oz.
  = 0.034 fl. oz.
  = 0.0022 lb.
  = 0.002 pt.
  = 0.001 l
  = 1000 mg
  = 0.001 kg

1 ounce (oz.) = 480 gr.
  = 28.35 gm
  = 0.0075 gal.
  = 0.03 qt.
  = 0.06 pt.
  = 0.0625 lb.
  = 0.96 fl. oz.

1 pound (lb.) = 5760 gr.
  = 373.24 gm

1 pound, avoirdupois = 7000 gr.
  = 453.6 gm
  = 16 oz.

LINEAR EQUIVALENTS

1 centimeter (cm) = 0.3937 in.
1 cubic centimeter (cm³) = 0.0610 in.³
1 cubic foot (ft.³) = 7,481 gal.
  = 29.922 qt.
  = 59.844 pt.
  = 62.426 lb.
  = 998.816 oz.
  = 957.51 fl. oz.
  = 1728 in.³
  = 28.32 l

1 cubic inch (in.³) = 16.387 cc or cm³
  = 0.0043 gal.
  = 0.017 qt.
  = 0.035 pt.
  = 0.036 lb.
  = 0.576 oz.
  = 0.554 fl. oz.

1 cubic meter (m³) = 35.314 ft.³
  = 61.024 in.³
  = 1000 l

PARTS PER MILLION (ppm)

1 ppm = 1 mg/l
  = 3.8 mg/gal.

= 2.7 lb./acre foot
= 0.0038 gm/gal.
= 0.0283 gm/ft.^{3}
= 1 oz./1000 ft.^{3}
= 0.0000623 lb./ft.^{3}
= 0.0586 gr./gal.
= 8.34 lb./million gal. water
= 0.134 oz./1000 gal.
= 1 oz./1000 ft.^{3} water
= gm/264 gal. water
= 1 gm/m^3 water

1 gr./gal. = 19.12 ppm

PERCENTAGE SOLUTIONS

1 percent solution = 38 gm/gal.
= 1.3 oz./gal.
= 10 gm/1000 ml
= 10 ml/1000 ml
= 10 ml/l
= 38 ml/gal.
= 1 gm/100 ml
= 1 oz./0.75 U.S. gal.
= 4.53 gm/lb.
= 0.624 lb./ft.^{3}

COMPUTING SIZE OF PUMP NEEDED FOR WATERFALL

1. Fill a one-gallon bucket with water.
2. Time the number of seconds required to empty the bucket for the desired flow over the waterfall.
3. Divide 60 by the number of seconds for the gallons per minute and then multiply by 60 for the number of gallons per hour (GPH) required to produce the desired flow.
4. Measure the height of the waterfall from the location of the pump in the pool. Round up to the nearest whole foot. Add an additional foot for every 10 feet of hosing that will be required to reach top of waterfall. This is the lift required of the pump.
5. Find the lift in feet on the chart below and follow down that column to match with the desired GPH. If the required GPH is not listed, select the pump at the next-highest GPH. Since most water gardening pumps are sized by the GPH at one foot of lift, the one-foot lift column will be the size of the pump. Larger sump pumps are sized by horsepower ratings.

LIFTS	1′	3′	5′	10′	15′	20′
	120	70				
	170	140	100			
GHP	205	168	120			
	300	255	205	70		
	325	300	270	130		
	500	435	337	210	65	
	600	580	517	414	230	90
	710	690	670	580	380	150
	810	790	745	613	415	173
	1200	1170	1100	1000	840	520
1/6 HP				900	690	480
0.3 HP				2750	1750	750
0.4 HP				3250	2500	1550

RECOMMENDED TUBING BORE FOR PUMPS TO WATERFALLS

½ inch diameter	for flows up to	120 GPH
¾ inch diameter	for flows up to	350 GPH
1 inch diameter	for flows up to	1000 GPH
1¼ inch diameter	for flows up to	1500 GPH
1½ inch diameter	for flows up to	3000 GPH

If the length of the tubing is longer than 10 to 15 feet, the next-larger size tubing should be used.

ACKNOWLEDGMENTS

A special thanks to the many people and companies who contributed both information and photos for this book. Their gracious sharing not only made my job easier, but also facilitates your job of pond maintenance.

Richard Schuck and Kelly Billings of Maryland Aquatic Nurseries in Maryland shared many time-saving tips, beautiful photos, and camera-ready drawings. Robert Johnson of Pond Care in Fresno, California, shared his special vision of water gardening, as did Cla Allgood of Allgood Outdoors in Georgia. Greg Maxwell of Maxwell Tree Service in Fort Wayne, Indiana, carried his camera to share time-saving ideas. Greg Speichert of Crystal Palace Perennials in St. John, Indiana, graciously shared many of his photographs of aquatic plants. Greg Jones of Waterfall Landscapes again shares beautiful designs combined with low maintenance. Little Giant Pump Corporation and E.G. Danner (manufacturer of Supreme Pumps) both shared photos of their products that lend ease to water gardening. Aquarium Pharmaceuticals and their James Layton shared many tips, information, and photos. George Rosicky of Leisure Bio Filters allowed us free rein to photograph his designs, both separately and in operation. Blue Ridge Fish Hatchery shared marvelous photos of fish, as did Nick Romanowski of Dragonfly Aquatics in Australia. The Kinsman Company willingly shared photos of low-maintenance landscaping ideas. Walkmaster Company kindly shared the entire sequence of constructing the cobble-look pathways. And Firehouse Image Center in Indianapolis allowed us to photograph their low-maintenance fountain.

Friends Henry and Carole Reimer of Reimer Waterscapes® in Ontario culled their many photos for the special ones needed for this book. T.J. Smith of my hometown, Logansport, Indiana, highlights the "ponds of Cass County" and many low-maintenance ideas designed by Joe and Lee Scheidler in the Hugh Leeman pond. Carole Christensen, a gifted professional photographer in the Atlanta, Georgia, area shared her talented visions. Brother-in-law Joe Cook revived a photography talent to help out, and dear friend and photographer of *The Pond Doctor* Ron Everhart shared more of his special interpretations. Steve Stroupe of Davis Creek Nursery in Alabama shared tips on growing aquatic plants. Betsy Sakata of Sakata Associates and the International Water Lily Society shared the Hawaiian touch. Marilyn Ahr of Buchanan, Tennessee, kindly sent along photos of her own low-maintenance pond. Carla Anderson in Colorado braved the attention of her German shepherd to photograph her pond and tools. Joe Tomocik of Denver Botanic Gardens gave up a lunch hour to find special slides. And Zionsville neighbors Bud Adkinson and Lynn Jenkins allowed us to photograph their creations.

Through the wonders of cyberspace, other pondkeepers shared their tips and designs. Steve Koeppel allowed us into the world of his backyard to see a UV filter unit in operation. Cliff Tallman in Michigan proved that retired school administrators can have other lives as he shared photography talent and design ideas. M.J. Girot of Arizona shared her fresh interpretation of a Mexican soapstone fountain, now a delightful water garden. Mary and Bob Kerns of Oregon, avid koi breeders and Trekkies, shared their unique and carefree filtration system. Dean Evans from Florida shared his design and experience with a goldfish lanai pond. Southerner Jan Noel-Smith shared tips to make maintenance easier. And Jim Martinson in Kansas shared the special designs and techniques he's discovered in water gardening.

I am especially thankful to my cousin Marcia Saatzer, who found the talented Lee Dreyfuss to photograph the koi pond inspiration of Jonathan Kellerman's Alex Delaware. A special thanks goes to Joe B. Dekker of New Jersey for again sharing his inexpensive design of skimmer filtration. And, certainly, a very warm thanks to the talented young photographer Oliver Jackson, who taught me much as he worked his camera magic.

INDEX